THE COMPLETE BEGINNERS GUIDE TO HOME CANNING

A STEP-BY-STEP GUIDE WITH 100 RECIPES FOR CANNING AND PRESERVING FOODS. LEARN THE PROPER METHODS OF WATER-PACKING AND PRESSURIZATION

Allan Smith

All rights reserved.

Disclaimer

The information contained in this eBook is meant to serve as a comprehensive collection of strategies that the author of this eBook has done research about. Summaries, strategies, tips, and tricks are only recommendations by the author, and reading this eBook will not guarantee that one's results will exactly mirror the author's results. The author of the eBook has made all reasonable efforts to provide current and accurate information for the readers of the eBook. The author and its associates will not be held liable for any unintentional error or omissions that may be found. The material in the eBook may include information by third parties. Third-party materials comprise opinions expressed by their owners. As such, the author of the eBook does not assume responsibility or liability for any third-party material or opinions. Whether because of the progression of the internet, or the unforeseen changes in company policy and editorial submission guidelines, what is stated as fact at the time of this writing may become outdated or inapplicable later.

The eBook is copyright © 2022 with all rights reserved. It is illegal to redistribute, copy, or create derivative work from this eBook whole or in part. No parts of this report may be reproduced or retransmitted in any reproduced or retransmitted in any forms whatsoever without the writing expressed and signed permission from the author.

TABLE OF CONTENTS

TABLE OF CONTENTS 3

INTRODUCTION 7

JAMS AND JELLIES 8

   1. STRAWBERRY-RHUBARB JAM 9
   2. NECTARINE-AND-SOUR CHERRY JAM 12
   3. LOW-SUGAR STRAWBERRY-TEQUILA AGAVE JAM 15
   4. CHOCOLATE-CHERRY JAM 17
   5. ORANGE-BANANA JAM 20
   6. APRICOT-LAVENDER JAM 22
   7. FIG-AND-PEAR JAM 25
   8. FIG, ROSEMARY, AND RED WINE JAM 28
   9. MELON JAM 31
   10. PEACH-ROSEMARY JAM 34
   11. HONEY-PEAR JAM 37
   12. APPLE PIE JAM 40
   13. PEACH-BOURBON JAM 43
   14. LOW-SUGAR RASPBERRY "LEMONADE" JAM 46
   15. TOMATO-HERB JAM 48
   16. ZUCCHINI-BREAD JAM 51
   17. BERRY-ALE JAM 54
   18. LOW-SUGAR APPLE-CHILE JAM 57
   19. BALSAMIC-ONION JAM 60
   20. BLUEBERRY-LEMON JAM 63
   21. APPLE JAM 66
   22. STRAWBERRY-RHUBARB JELLY 68
   23. BLUEBERRY-SPICE JAM 70
   24. GRAPE-PLUM JELLY 72

25. GOLDEN PEPPER JELLY 75
26. PEACH-PINEAPPLE SPREAD 78
27. REFRIGERATED APPLE SPREAD 81
28. REFRIGERATOR GRAPE SPREAD 83
29. APPLE JELLY WITHOUT ADDED PECTIN 85
30. APPLE MARMALADE WITHOUT ADDED PECTIN 87
31. BLACKBERRY JELLY WITHOUT ADDED PECTIN 89
32. CHERRY JELLY WITH POWDERED PECTIN 91
33. CHERRY JAM WITH POWDERED PECTIN 93
34. FIG JAM WITH LIQUID PECTIN 95
35. GRAPE JELLY WITH POWDERED PECTIN 97
36. MINT-PINEAPPLE JAM WITH LIQUID PECTIN 99
37. MIXED FRUIT JELLY WITH LIQUID PECTIN 101
38. ORANGE JELLY 104
39. SPICED ORANGE JELLY 106
40. ORANGE MARMALADE 109
41. APRICOT-ORANGE CONSERVE 112
42. PEACH JAM WITH POWDERED PECTIN 114
43. SPICED BLUEBERRY-PEACH JAM 116
44. PEACH-ORANGE MARMALADE 119
45. PINEAPPLE JAM WITH LIQUID PECTIN 121
46. PLUM JELLY WITH LIQUID PECTIN 123
47. QUINCE JELLY WITHOUT ADDED PECTIN 125
48. STRAWBERRY JAM WITH POWDERED PECTIN 127
49. TUTTI-FRUTTI JAM 129

FRUIT AND FRUIT PRODUCTS 132

50. APPLE BUTTER 133
51. SPICED APPLE RINGS 135
52. SPICED CRAB APPLES 138
53. CANTALOUPE PICKLES 141

54. Cranberry orange chutney 144

55. Mango chutney 147

56. Mango sauce 150

57. Mixed fruit cocktail 153

58. Zucchini-pineapple 156

59. Spicy cranberry salsa 158

60. Mango salsa 161

61. Peach apple salsa 164

FERMENTED AND PICKLED VEGETABLES 167

62. Dill pickles 168

63. Sauerkraut 171

64. Bread-and-butter pickles 174

65. Fresh-pack dill pickles 177

66. Sweet gherkin pickles 180

67. 14-Day sweet pickles 183

68. Quick sweet pickles 186

69. Pickled asparagus 189

70. Pickled dilled beans 192

71. Pickled three-bean salad 194

72. Pickled beets 197

73. Pickled carrots 200

74. Pickled cauliflower/Brussels 203

75. Chayote and jicama slaw 206

76. Bread-and-butter pickled jicama 209

77. Marinated whole mushrooms 211

78. Pickled dilled okra 214

79. Pickled pearl onions 216

80. Marinated peppers 219

81. Pickled bell peppers 222

82. Pickled hot peppers 225

83. Pickled Jalapeño Pepper Rings 228
84. Pickled yellow pepper rings 231
85. Pickled sweet green tomatoes. 233
86. Pickled mixed vegetables 236
87. Pickled bread-and-butter zucchini 239
88. Chayote and pear relish 241
89. Piccalilli 244
90. Pickle relish 247
91. Pickled corn relish 250
92. Pickled green tomato relish 253
93. Pickled horseradish sauce 256
94. Pickled pepper-onion relish 258
95. Spicy jicama relish 260
96. Tangy tomatillo relish 263
97. No sugar added pickled beets 266
98. Sweet pickle cucumber 269
99. Sliced dill pickles 272
100. Sliced sweet pickles 275

CONCLUSION 278

INTRODUCTION

Home canning has changed greatly in the 180 years since it was introduced as a way to preserve food. Scientists have found ways to produce safer, higher quality products. The first part of this publication explains the scientific principles on which canning techniques are based, discusses canning equipment, and describes the proper use of jars and lids. It describes basic canning ingredients and procedures and how to use them to achieve safe, high-quality canned products. Finally, it helps you decide whether or not and how much to can.

The second part of this publication is a series of canning guides for specific foods. These guides offer detailed directions for making sugar syrups; and for canning fruits and fruit products, tomatoes and tomato products, vegetables, red meats, poultry, seafood, and pickles and relishes. Handy guidelines for choosing the right quantities and quality of raw foods accompany each set of directions for fruits, tomatoes, and vegetables. Most recipes are designed to yield a full canner load of pints or quarts. Finally, processing adjustments for altitudes above sea level are given for each food.

JAMS AND JELLIES

1. Strawberry-rhubarb jam

MAKES ABOUT 6 (½-PT./250-ML) JARS

Ingredients

- 4½ cups (1.1 L) ¼-inch (.5-cm)-thick sliced fresh rhubarb
- ½ cup (125 mL) fresh orange juice (about 2 to 3 large oranges)
- 4 cups (1 L) ripe fresh strawberries
- 5 cups (1.25 L) sugar
- 1 (3-oz./88.5-mL) pouch Ball® Liquid Pectin

Directions:

a) Combine rhubarb and orange juice in a 3-qt. (3-L) stainless steel saucepan. Cover and bring to a boil over medium-high heat. Uncover, reduce heat, and simmer, stirring often, 5 minutes or until rhubarb is tender.

b) Wash strawberries; remove and discard stems and hulls. Mash strawberries with a potato masher until evenly crushed.

c) Measure 2 cups (500 mL) cooked rhubarb and 1¾ cups (425 mL) mashed strawberries into a 6-qt. (6-L) stainless steel or enameled Dutch oven. Stir in sugar. Bring mixture to a full rolling boil that cannot be stirred down, over high heat, stirring frequently.

d) Add pectin, immediately squeezing entire contents from pouch. Continue hard boil for 1 minute, stirring constantly. Remove from heat. Skim foam, if necessary.

e) Ladle hot jam into a hot jar, leaving $\frac{1}{4}$-inch (.5-cm) headspace. Remove air bubbles. Wipe jar rim. Center lid on jar. Apply band, and adjust to fingertip-tight. Place jar in boiling-water canner. Repeat until all jars are filled.

f) Process jars 10 minutes, adjusting for altitude. Turn off heat; remove lid, and let jars stand 5 minutes. Remove jars and cool.

2. Nectarine-and-sour cherry jam

MAKES ABOUT 7 (½-PT./250-ML) JARS

Ingredients

- 1½ lb. (750 g) nectarines, pitted and finely chopped
- 2 cups (500 mL) chopped pitted tart cherries
- 6 Tbsp. (90 mL) Ball® Classic Pectin
- 2 Tbsp. (30 mL) bottled lemon juice
- 6 cups (1.5 L) sugar

Directions:

a) Combine first 4 ingredients in a 4-qt. (4-L) stainless steel or enameled Dutch oven. Bring mixture to a full rolling boil that cannot be stirred down, over high heat, stirring constantly.

b) Add sugar, stirring to dissolve. Return mixture to a full rolling boil. Boil hard 1 minute, stirring constantly. Remove from heat. Skim foam, if necessary.

c) Ladle hot jam into a hot jar, leaving ¼-inch (.5-cm) headspace. Remove air bubbles. Wipe jar rim. Center lid on jar. Apply band, and adjust to fingertip-tight. Place jar in boiling-water canner. Repeat until all jars are filled.

d) Process jars 10 minutes, adjusting for altitude. Turn off heat; remove lid, and let jars stand 5 minutes. Remove jars and cool.

3. Low-sugar strawberry-tequila agave jam

MAKES ABOUT 4 (½-PT./250 ML) JARS

Ingredients

- 5 cups (1.25 L) chopped fresh strawberries
- ½ cup (125 mL) tequila
- 5 Tbsp. (75 mL) Ball® Low or No-Sugar Pectin
- 1 cup (250 mL) agave syrup

Directions:

a) Combine first 2 ingredients in a 4-qt. (4-L) stainless steel or enameled Dutch oven. Crush berries with a potato masher.

b) Stir in pectin. Bring mixture to a full rolling boil that cannot be stirred down, over high heat, stirring constantly.

c) Stir in agave syrup. Return mixture to a full rolling boil. Boil hard 1 minute, stirring constantly. Remove from heat. Skim foam, if necessary.

d) Ladle hot jam into a hot jar, leaving ¼-inch (.5-cm) headspace. Remove air bubbles. Wipe jar rim. Center lid on jar. Apply band, and adjust to fingertip-tight. Place jar in boiling-water canner. Repeat until all jars are filled.

e) Process jars 10 minutes, adjusting for altitude. Turn off heat; remove lid, and let jars stand 5 minutes. Remove jars and cool.

4. Chocolate-cherry jam

MAKES ABOUT 6 (½-PT./250-ML) JARS

Ingredients

- 6 cups (1.5 L) fresh or frozen pitted dark, sweet cherries, coarsely chopped
- 6 Tbsp. (90 mL) Ball® Classic Pectin
- ¼ cup (60 mL) bottled lemon juice
- 6 cups (1.5 L) sugar
- ⅔ cup (150 mL) unsweetened cocoa

Directions:

a) Combine first 3 ingredients in a 4-qt. (4-L) stainless steel or enameled Dutch oven. Bring mixture to a full rolling boil that cannot be stirred down, over high heat, stirring constantly.

b) Meanwhile, stir together sugar and cocoa until blended; add all at once to boiling cherry mixture. Return mixture to a full rolling boil. Boil hard 1 minute, stirring constantly. Remove from heat. Skim foam, if necessary.

c) Ladle hot jam into a hot jar, leaving ¼-inch (.5-cm) headspace. Remove air bubbles. Wipe jar rim. Center lid on jar. Apply band, and adjust to fingertip-tight. Place jar in boiling-water canner. Repeat until all jars are filled.

d) Process jars 10 minutes, adjusting for altitude. Turn off heat; remove lid, and let jars stand 5 minutes. Remove jars and cool.

5. Orange-banana jam

MAKES ABOUT 5 (½-PT./250-ML) JARS

Ingredients

- 2 cups (500 mL) fresh orange juice with pulp (about 8 oranges)
- 1 cup (250 mL) honey
- 3 Tbsp. (45 mL) bottled lemon juice
- 2 lb. (1 kg) very ripe bananas, peeled and chopped
- 1 vanilla bean, split

Directions:

a) Combine first 4 ingredients in a 4-qt. (4-L) stainless steel or enameled Dutch oven. Scrape seeds from vanilla bean; add to banana mixture. Cook, stirring often, over medium heat for about 25 minutes to gelling point.

b) Ladle hot jam into a hot jar, leaving $\frac{1}{4}$-inch (.5-cm) headspace. Remove air bubbles. Wipe jar rim. Center lid on jar. Apply band, and adjust to fingertip-tight. Place jar in boiling-water canner. Repeat until all jars are filled.

c) Process jars 15 minutes, adjusting for altitude. Turn off heat; remove lid, and let jars stand 5 minutes. Remove jars and cool.

6. Apricot-lavender jam

MAKES ABOUT 6 (½-PT./250-ML) JARS

Ingredients

- 4 tsp. (20 mL) dried lavender buds
- Cheesecloth
- Kitchen string
- 3 lb. (1.5 kg) apricots, pitted and chopped (about 6 cups/1.5 L)
- 4 cups (1 L) sugar
- 3 Tbsp. (45 mL) bottled lemon juice

Directions:

a) Place lavender buds on a 4-inch (10-cm) square of cheesecloth; tie with kitchen string.

b) Place apricots in a large bowl; mash with a potato masher until crushed. Stir in sugar and lemon juice; add cheesecloth bag, stirring until moistened. Cover and chill 4 hours or overnight.

c) Pour apricot mixture into a 6-qt. (6-L) stainless steel or enameled Dutch oven. Bring to a boil over medium heat, stirring until sugar dissolves. Increase heat to medium-high. Cook, stirring constantly, 45 minutes or until mixture is thickened and a candy thermometer registers 220°F

(104°C). Remove from heat. Remove and discard cheesecloth bag.

d) Ladle hot jam into a hot jar, leaving $\frac{1}{4}$-inch (.5-cm) headspace. Remove air bubbles. Wipe jar rim. Center lid on jar. Apply band, and adjust to fingertip-tight. Place jar in boiling-water canner. Repeat until all jars are filled.

e) Process jars 10 minutes, adjusting for altitude. Turn off heat; remove lid, and let jars stand 5 minutes. Remove jars and cool.

7. Fig-and-pear jam

MAKES ABOUT 4 (½-PT./250 ML) JARS

Ingredients

- 2 cups (250 mL) chopped pears
- 2 cups (250 mL) chopped fresh figs
- 4 Tbsp. (60 mL) Ball® Classic Pectin
- 2 Tbsp. (30 mL) bottled lemon juice
- 1 Tbsp. (15 mL) water
- 3 cups (750 mL) sugar

Directions:

a) Combine all ingredients, except sugar, in a 4-qt. (4-L) stainless steel or enameled Dutch oven. Bring mixture to a full rolling boil that cannot be stirred down, over high heat, stirring constantly.

b) Add sugar, stirring to dissolve. Return mixture to a full rolling boil. Boil hard 1 minute, stirring constantly. Remove from heat. Skim foam, if necessary.

c) Ladle hot jam into a hot jar, leaving ¼-inch (.5-cm) headspace. Wipe jar rim. Center lid on jar. Apply band, and adjust to fingertip-tight. Place jar in boiling-water canner. Repeat until all jars are filled.

d) Process jars 10 minutes, adjusting for altitude. Turn off heat; remove lid, and let jars stand 5 minutes. Remove jars and cool.

8. Fig, rosemary, and red wine jam

MAKES ABOUT 4 (½-PT./250-ML) JARS

Ingredients

- 1½ cups (375 mL) Merlot or other fruity red wine
- 2 Tbsp. (30 mL) fresh rosemary leaves
- 2 cups (500 mL) finely chopped fresh figs
- 3 Tbsp. (45 mL) Ball® Classic Pectin
- 2 Tbsp. (30 mL) bottled lemon juice
- 2½ cups (625 mL) sugar

Directions:

a) Bring wine and rosemary to a simmer in a small stainless steel or enameled saucepan. Turn off heat; cover and steep 30 minutes.

b) Pour wine through a fine wire-mesh strainer into a 4-qt. (4-L) stainless steel or enameled saucepan. Discard rosemary. Stir in figs, pectin, and lemon juice. Bring mixture to a full rolling boil that cannot be stirred down, over high heat, stirring constantly.

c) Add sugar, stirring to dissolve. Return mixture to a full rolling boil. Boil hard 1 minute, stirring constantly. Remove from heat. Skim foam, if necessary.

d) Ladle hot jam into a hot jar, leaving $\frac{1}{4}$-inch (.5-cm) headspace. Remove air bubbles. Wipe jar rim. Center lid on jar. Apply band, and adjust to fingertip-tight. Place jar in boiling-water canner. Repeat until all jars are filled.

e) Process jars 10 minutes, adjusting for altitude. Turn off heat; remove lid, and let jars stand 5 minutes. Remove jars and cool.

9. Melon jam

MAKES ABOUT 5 (½-PT./250-ML) JARS

Ingredients

- 14 cups (3.5 L) 1-inch (1-cm) cantaloupe or other orange-fleshed melon cubes (about 2 large melons)
- ¼ cup (60 mL) kosher salt
- 4 cups (1 L) sugar
- ¾ cup (175 mL) bottled lemon juice
- 1 Tbsp. (15 mL) crushed pink peppercorns (optional)

Directions:

a) Toss together melon and salt in a large bowl. Cover and let stand 2 hours. Drain; rinse with cold water. Drain.

b) Stir together melon, sugar, and lemon juice in a 6-qt. (6-L) stainless steel or enameled Dutch oven. Bring to a boil; reduce heat, and simmer, uncovered, 20 minutes or until melon is soft. Mash melon pieces with a potato masher. Simmer, uncovered, stirring often, about 1 hour to gelling point. (Melons release a lot of water, so cooking time may vary.) Skim foam, if necessary, and, if desired, stir in peppercorns.

c) Ladle hot jam into a hot jar, leaving ¼-inch (.5-cm) headspace. Remove air bubbles. Wipe jar rim. Center lid on

jar. Apply band, and adjust to fingertip-tight. Place jar in boiling-water canner. Repeat until all jars are filled.

d) Process jars 15 minutes, adjusting for altitude. Turn off heat; remove lid, and let jars stand 5 minutes. Remove jars and cool.

10. Peach-rosemary jam

MAKES ABOUT 6 (½-PT./250 ML) JARS

Ingredients

- 2½ lb. (1.25 kg) fresh peaches (5 large)
- 1 tsp. (5 mL) lime zest
- 6 Tbsp. (90 mL) Ball® Classic Pectin
- ¼ cup (60 mL) fresh lime juice (about 3 limes)
- 2 (4-inch/10-cm) rosemary sprigs
- 5 cups (1.25 L) sugar

Directions:

a) Peel peaches with a vegetable peeler. Remove pits, and coarsely chop. Mash with a potato masher until evenly crushed. Measure 4 cups (1 L) crushed peaches into a 6-qt. (6-L) stainless steel or enameled Dutch oven. Stir in lime zest and next 3 ingredients.

b) Bring mixture to a full rolling boil that cannot be stirred down, over high heat, stirring constantly. Boil 1 minute, stirring constantly.

c) Add sugar, stirring to dissolve. Return mixture to a full rolling boil. Boil hard 1 minute, stirring constantly. Remove from heat. Remove and discard rosemary. Skim foam, if necessary.

d) Ladle hot jam into a hot jar, leaving $\frac{1}{4}$-inch (.5-cm) headspace. Remove air bubbles. Wipe jar rim. Center lid on jar. Apply band, and adjust to fingertip-tight. Place jar in boiling-water canner. Repeat until all jars are filled.

e) Process jars 10 minutes, adjusting for altitude. Turn off heat; remove lid, and let jars stand 5 minutes. Remove jars and cool.

11. Honey-pear jam

MAKES ABOUT 5 (½-PT./250-ML) JARS

Ingredients

- 3¼ lb. (1.5 kg) firm, ripe pears
- ½ cup (125 mL) apple juice
- 1 Tbsp. (15 mL) bottled lemon juice
- ½ tsp. (2.5 mL) ground cinnamon
- 1-piece fresh ginger, peeled and finely grated
- 6 Tbsp. (90 mL) Ball® Low or No-Sugar Pectin
- ½ cup (125 mL) honey

Directions:

a) Combine first 5 ingredients in a 6-qt. (6-L) stainless steel or enameled Dutch oven. Cook, uncovered, over medium heat 15 minutes or until pear is tender, stirring occasionally. Mash pear mixture slightly with a potato masher, breaking up large chunks.

b) Stir in pectin. Bring mixture to a full rolling boil that cannot be stirred down, over high heat, stirring constantly.

c) Stir in honey. Return mixture to a full rolling boil. Boil hard 1 minute, stirring constantly. Remove from heat. Skim foam, if necessary.

d) Ladle hot jam into a hot jar, leaving $\frac{1}{4}$-inch (.5-cm) headspace. Remove air bubbles. Wipe jar rim. Center lid on jar. Apply band, and adjust to fingertip-tight. Place jar in boiling-water canner. Repeat until all jars are filled.

e) Process jars 10 minutes, adjusting for altitude. Turn off heat; remove lid, and let jars stand 5 minutes. Remove jars and cool.

12. Apple pie jam

MAKES ABOUT 5 (½-PT./250-ML) JARS

Ingredients

- 6 cups (1.5 L) diced peeled Granny Smith apple (about 6 apples)
- 2 cups (500 mL) apple juice or apple cider
- 2 Tbsp. (30 mL) bottled lemon juice
- 3 Tbsp. (45 mL) Ball® Classic Pectin
- 1 tsp. (5 mL) ground cinnamon
- ½ tsp. (2 mL) ground allspice
- ¼ tsp. (1 mL) ground nutmeg
- 2 cups (500 mL) sugar

Directions:

a) Bring first 3 ingredients to a boil in a 6-qt. (6-L) stainless steel or enameled Dutch oven; reduce heat, and simmer, uncovered, 10 minutes or until apple is soft, stirring occasionally.

b) Whisk in pectin and next 3 ingredients. Bring mixture to a full rolling boil that cannot be stirred down, over high heat, stirring constantly.

c) Add sugar, stirring to dissolve. Return mixture to a full rolling boil. Boil hard 1 minute, stirring constantly. Remove from heat. Skim foam, if necessary.

d) Ladle hot jam into a hot jar, leaving $\frac{1}{4}$-inch (.5-cm) headspace. Remove air bubbles. Wipe jar rim. Center lid on jar. Apply band, and adjust to fingertip-tight. Place jar in boiling-water canner. Repeat until all jars are filled.

e) Process jars 10 minutes, adjusting for altitude. Turn off heat; remove lid, and let jars stand 5 minutes. Remove jars and cool.

13. Peach-bourbon jam

MAKES ABOUT 6 (½-PT./250-ML) JARS

Ingredients

- 4 lb. (2 kg) fresh peaches, peeled
- 6 Tbsp. (90 mL) Ball® Classic Pectin
- ¼ cup (60 mL) bottled lemon juice
- ¼ cup (60 mL) bourbon
- 2 Tbsp. (30 mL) finely chopped crystallized ginger
- 7 cups (1.75 L) sugar

Directions:

a) Pit and coarsely chop peaches. Measure 4½ cups (1.1 L) chopped peaches into a 6-qt. (6-L) stainless steel or enameled Dutch oven, and mash with a potato masher until evenly crushed. Stir in pectin and next 3 ingredients.

b) Bring mixture to a full rolling boil that cannot be stirred down, over high heat, stirring constantly.

c) Add sugar, stirring to dissolve. Return mixture to a full rolling boil. Boil hard 1 minute, stirring constantly. Remove from heat. Skim foam, if necessary.

d) Ladle hot jam into a hot jar, leaving ¼-inch (.5-cm) headspace. Remove air bubbles. Wipe jar rim. Center lid on

jar. Apply band, and adjust to fingertip-tight. Place jar in boiling-water canner. Repeat until all jars are filled.

e) Process jars 10 minutes, adjusting for altitude. Turn off heat; remove lid, and let jars stand 5 minutes. Remove jars and cool.

14. Low-sugar raspberry "lemonade" jam

MAKES ABOUT 6 (½-PT./250-ML) JARS

Ingredients

- 3½ lb. (1.6 kg) fresh raspberries
- ½ cup (125 mL) fresh lemon juice (about 5 lemons)
- 4 Tbsp. (60 mL) Ball® Low or No-Sugar Pectin
- 1½ cups (375 mL) honey

Directions:

a) Place raspberries in a 6-qt. (6-L) stainless steel or enameled Dutch oven. Crush raspberries with a potato masher.

b) Stir in lemon juice and pectin. Bring mixture to a full rolling boil that cannot be stirred down, over high heat, stirring constantly.

c) Stir in honey. Return mixture to a full rolling boil. Boil hard 1 minute, stirring constantly. Remove from heat. Skim foam, if necessary.

d) Ladle hot jam into a hot jar, leaving ¼-inch (.5-mL) headspace. Remove air bubbles. Wipe jar rim. Center lid on jar. Apply band, and adjust to fingertip-tight. Place jar in boiling-water canner. Repeat until all jars are filled.

e) Process jars 10 minutes, adjusting for altitude. Turn off heat; remove lid, and let jars stand 5 minutes. Remove jars and cool.

15. Tomato-herb jam

MAKES ABOUT 4 (½-PT./250-ML) JARS

Ingredients

- 6 lb. (3 kg) plum tomatoes, cored and chopped
- 1 tsp. (5 mL) salt
- ½ tsp. (2 mL) freshly ground black pepper
- 3 garlic cloves, minced
- 2 bay leaves
- 1½ cups (375 mL) sugar
- ½ cup (125 mL) balsamic vinegar
- ¼ cup (60 mL) dry white wine
- 2 tsp. (10 mL) herbes de Provence

Directions:

a) Combine first 5 ingredients in a 6-qt. (6-L) stainless steel or enameled Dutch oven. Cook, uncovered, over medium-high heat 1 hour or until reduced by half, stirring often.

b) Stir in sugar and next 3 ingredients. Cook, uncovered, over medium heat 45 minutes or until very thick, stirring occasionally. Remove and discard bay leaves.

c) Ladle hot jam into a hot jar, leaving ¼-inch (.5 mL) headspace. Remove air bubbles. Wipe jar rim. Center lid on

jar. Apply band, and adjust to fingertip-tight. Place jar in boiling-water canner. Repeat until all jars are filled.

d) Process jars 10 minutes, adjusting for altitude. Turn off heat; remove lid, and let jars stand 5 minutes. Remove jars and cool.

16. Zucchini-bread jam

MAKES ABOUT 4 (½-PT./250-ML) JARS

Ingredients

- 4 cups (1 L) shredded zucchini
- 1 cup (250 mL) apple juice
- 6 Tbsp. (90 mL) Ball® Classic Pectin
- ¼ cup (60 mL) golden raisins
- 1 Tbsp. (15 mL) bottled lemon juice
- 1 tsp. (5 mL) ground cinnamon
- ½ tsp. (2 mL) ground nutmeg
- 3 cups (750 mL) sugar

Directions:

a) Combine all ingredients, except sugar, in a 6-qt. (6-L) stainless steel or enameled Dutch oven. Bring mixture to a full rolling boil that cannot be stirred down, over high heat, stirring constantly.

b) Add sugar, stirring to dissolve. Return mixture to a full rolling boil. Boil hard 1 minute, stirring constantly. Remove from heat. Skim foam, if necessary.

c) Ladle hot jam into a hot jar, leaving ¼-inch (.5-cm) headspace. Remove air bubbles. Wipe jar rim. Center lid on

jar. Apply band, and adjust to fingertip-tight. Place jar in boiling-water canner. Repeat until all jars are filled.

d) Process jars 15 minutes, adjusting for altitude. Turn off heat; remove lid, and let jars stand 5 minutes. Remove jars and cool.

17. Berry-ale jam

MAKES ABOUT 6 (½-PT./250-ML) JARS

Ingredients

- 2 cups (500 mL) raspberries, blueberries, or strawberries
- 2 (12-oz./355-mL) bottles flat pale ale
- 6 Tbsp. (90 mL) Ball® Classic Pectin
- 1 tsp. (5 mL) lemon zest
- 2 Tbsp. (30 mL) fresh lemon juice
- 4 cups (1 L) sugar

Directions:

a) Place berries in a 6-qt. (6-L) stainless steel or enameled Dutch oven. Crush berries with a potato masher. Stir in ale and next 3 ingredients. Bring mixture to a full rolling boil that cannot be stirred down, over high heat, stirring constantly.

b) Add sugar, stirring to dissolve. Return mixture to a full rolling boil. Boil hard 1 minute, stirring constantly. Remove from heat. Skim foam, if necessary.

c) Ladle hot jam into a hot jar, leaving ¼-inch (.5-cm) headspace. Remove air bubbles. Wipe jar rim. Center lid on jar. Apply band, and adjust to fingertip-tight. Place jar in boiling-water canner. Repeat until all jars are filled.

d) Process jars 10 minutes, adjusting for altitude. Turn off heat; remove lid, and let jars stand 5 minutes. Remove jars and cool.

18. Low-sugar apple-chile jam

MAKES ABOUT 5 (½-PT./250-ML) JARS

Ingredients

- 2 large apples (about 8½ oz./480 g, each), peeled and grated
- 3 Tbsp. (45 mL) bottled lemon juice
- 4 cups (1 L) apple juice
- 3 Tbsp. (45 mL) Ball® Low or No-Sugar Pectin
- 1 Tbsp. (15 mL) crushed chile de árbol, or dried crushed red pepper
- ½ cup (125 mL) sugar
- ½ cup (125 mL) honey

Directions:

a) Combine grated apple and lemon juice in a 4-qt. (4-L) stainless steel or enameled Dutch oven. Cook, stirring constantly, 10 minutes or until apple is tender.

b) Stir in apple juice, pectin, and crushed chile de árbol. Bring mixture to a full rolling boil that cannot be stirred down, over high heat, stirring constantly.

c) Add sugar and honey, stirring to dissolve sugar. Return mixture to a full rolling boil. Boil hard 1 minute, stirring constantly. Remove from heat. Skim foam, if necessary.

d) Ladle hot jam into a hot jar, leaving $\frac{1}{4}$-inch (.5-cm) headspace. Remove air bubbles. Wipe jar rim. Center lid on jar. Apply band, and adjust to fingertip-tight. Place jar in boiling-water canner. Repeat until all jars are filled.

e) Process jars 10 minutes, adjusting for altitude. Turn off heat; remove lid, and let jars stand 5 minutes. Remove jars and cool.

19. Balsamic-onion jam

MAKES ABOUT 5 (½-PT./250-ML) JARS

Ingredients

- 2 lb. (1 kg) onions, diced
- ½ cup (125 mL) balsamic vinegar
- ½ cup (125 mL) maple syrup
- 1½ tsp. (7.5 mL) salt
- 2 tsp. (10 mL) ground white pepper
- 1 bay leaf
- 2 cups (500 mL) apple juice
- 3 Tbsp. (45 mL) Ball® Low or No-Sugar Pectin
- ½ cup (125 mL) sugar

Directions:

a) Combine first 6 ingredients in a 6-qt. (6-L) stainless steel or enameled Dutch oven. Cook over medium heat 15 minutes or until onions are translucent, stirring occasionally.

b) Stir in apple juice and pectin. Bring mixture to a full rolling boil that cannot be stirred down, over high heat, stirring constantly.

c) Add sugar, stirring to dissolve. Return mixture to a full rolling boil. Boil hard 1 minute, stirring constantly. Remove from heat. Remove and discard bay leaf. Skim foam, if necessary.

d) Ladle hot jam into a hot jar, leaving $\frac{1}{4}$-inch (.5-cm) headspace. Remove air bubbles. Wipe jar rim. Center lid on jar. Apply band, and adjust to fingertip-tight. Place jar in boiling-water canner. Repeat until all jars are filled.

e) Process jars 15 minutes, adjusting for altitude. Turn off heat; remove lid, and let jars stand 5 minutes. Remove jars and cool.

20. Blueberry-lemon jam

MAKES ABOUT 4 (½-PT./250-ML) JARS

Ingredients

- 4 cups (1 L) fresh blueberries
- 3½ cups (1.6 L) sugar
- 1 tsp. (5 mL) lemon zest
- 1 Tbsp. (15 mL) fresh lemon juice
- 1 (3-oz./88.5-mL) pouch Ball® Liquid Pectin

Directions:

a) Wash, drain, and lightly crush blueberries with a spoon (just enough to split the skins). Measure 2½ cups (625 mL) crushed blueberries into a 6-qt. (6-L) stainless steel or enameled Dutch oven.

b) Add sugar and next 2 ingredients. Bring mixture to a full rolling boil that cannot be stirred down, over high heat, stirring constantly.

c) Add pectin, immediately squeezing entire contents from pouch. Continue hard boil for 1 minute, stirring constantly. Remove from heat. Skim foam, if necessary.

d) Ladle hot mixture into a hot jar, leaving ¼-inch (.5-cm) headspace. Remove air bubbles. Wipe jar rim. Center lid on jar. Apply band, and adjust to fingertip-tight. Place jar in boiling-water canner. Repeat until all jars are filled.

e) Process jars 10 minutes, adjusting for altitude. Turn off heat; remove lid, and let jars stand 5 minutes. Remove jars and cool.

21. Apple jam

Ingredients:

- 2 cups peeled, cored, and chopped pears
- 1 cup peeled, cored, and chopped apples
- 6-1/2 cups sugar
- 1/4 teaspoons ground cinnamon
- 1/3 cup bottled lemon juice
- 6 oz. liquid pectin

Directions:

a) Crush apples and pears in a large saucepan and stir in cinnamon.

b) Thoroughly mix sugar and lemon juice with fruits and bring to a boil over high heat, stirring constantly. Immediately stir in pectin. Bring to a full rolling boil and boil hard 1 minute, stirring constantly.

c) Remove from heat, quickly skim off foam, and fill sterile jars leaving 1/4-inch headspace. Wipe rims of jars with a dampened clean paper towel.

d) Adjust lids and process.

22. Strawberry-rhubarb jelly

Ingredients:

- 1-1/2 lbs. red stalks of rhubarb
- 1-1/2 quarts' ripe strawberries
- 1/2 teaspoons butter or margarine to reduce foaming
- 6 cups sugar
- 6 oz. liquid pectin

Directions:

a) Wash and cut rhubarb into 1-inch pieces and blend or grind. Wash, stem, and crush strawberries, one layer at a time, in a saucepan.

b) Place both fruits in a jelly bag or double layer of cheesecloth and gently squeeze out juice. Measure 3-1/2 cups of juice into a large saucepan. Add butter and sugar, thoroughly mixing into juice.

c) Bring to a boil over high heat, stirring constantly. Immediately stir in pectin. Bring to a full rolling boil and boil hard 1 minute, stirring constantly.

d) Remove from heat, quickly skim off foam, and fill sterile jars, leaving 1/4-inch headspace. Wipe rims of jars with a dampened clean paper towel.

e) Adjust lids and process.

23. Blueberry-spice jam

Ingredients:

- 2-1/2 pints ripe blueberries
- 1 Tablespoon lemon juice
- 1/2 teaspoons ground nutmeg or cinnamon
- 5-1/2 cups sugar
- 3/4 cup water
- 1 box (1-3/4 oz.) powdered pectin

Directions:

a) Wash and thoroughly crush blueberries, one layer at a time, in a saucepan. Add lemon juice, spice, and water. Stir in pectin and bring to a full rolling boil over high heat, stirring frequently.

b) Add the sugar and return to a full rolling boil. Boil hard for 1 minute, stirring constantly.

c) Remove from heat, quickly skim off foam, and fill sterile jars, leaving 1/4-inch headspace. Wipe rims of jars with a dampened clean paper towel.

d) Adjust lids and process.

24. Grape-plum jelly

Ingredients:

- 3-1/2 lbs. ripe plums
- 3 lbs. ripe Concord grapes
- 1 cup water
- 1/2 teaspoons butter or margarine to reduce foaming (optional)
- 8-1/2 cups sugar
- 1 box (1-3/4 oz.) powdered pectin

Directions:

a) Wash and pit plums; do not peel. Thoroughly crush the plums and grapes, one layer at a time, in a saucepan with water. Bring to a boil, cover, and simmer 10 minutes.

b) Strain juice through a jelly bag or double layer of cheesecloth. Measure sugar and set aside.

c) Combine 6-1/2 cups of juice with butter and pectin in large saucepan. Bring to a hard boil over high heat, stirring constantly. Add the sugar and return to a full rolling boil. Boil hard for 1 minute, stirring constantly.

d) Remove from heat, quickly skim off foam, and fill sterile jars, leaving 1/4-inch headspace. Wipe rims of jars with a dampened clean paper towel.

e) Adjust lids and process.

25. Golden pepper jelly

Ingredients:

- 5 cups chopped yellow bell peppers
- ½ cup chopped Serrano chile peppers
- 1-1/2 cups white distilled vinegar (5%)
- 5 cups sugar
- 1 pouch (3 oz.) liquid pectin

Directions:

a) Wash all peppers thoroughly; remove stems and seeds from the peppers. Place sweet and hot peppers in a blender or food processor.

b) Add enough of the vinegar to puree the peppers, then puree. Combine the pepper-vinegar puree and remaining vinegar into an 8- or 10-quart saucepan. Heat to a boil; then boil 10 minutes to extract flavors and color.

c) Remove from heat and strain through a jelly bag into a bowl. (The jelly bag is preferred; several layers of cheesecloth may also be used.)

d) Measure 2-1/4 cups of the strained pepper-vinegar juice back into the saucepan. Stir in sugar until dissolved and return mixture to a boil. Add the pectin, return to a full rolling boil and boil hard for 1 minute, stirring constantly.

e) Remove from heat, quickly skim off any foam, and fill into sterile jars, leaving 1/4-inch headspace. Wipe rims of jars with a dampened clean paper towel.

f) Adjust lids and process.

26. Peach-pineapple spread

Ingredients:

- 4 cups drained peach pulp
- 2 cups drained unsweetened crushed pineapple
- 1/4 cup bottled lemon juice
- 2 cups sugar (optional)

Directions:

a) Thoroughly wash 4 to 6 pounds of firm, ripe peaches. Drain well. Peel and remove pits. Grind fruit flesh with a medium or coarse blade, or crush with a fork (do not use a blender).

b) Place ground or crushed fruit in a 2-quart saucepan. Heat slowly to release juice, stirring constantly, until fruit is tender.

c) Place cooked fruit in a jelly bag or strainer lined with four layers of cheesecloth. Allow juice to drip about 15 minutes. Save the juice for jelly or other uses.

d) Measure 4 cups of drained fruit pulp for making spread. Combine the 4 cups of pulp, pineapple, and lemon juice in a 4-quart saucepan. Add up to 2 cups of sugar, if desired, and mix well. Heat and boil gently for 10 to 15 minutes, stirring enough to prevent sticking.

e) Fill hot jars quickly, leaving 1/4-inch headspace. Wipe rims of jars with a dampened clean paper towel.

f) Adjust lids and process.

27. Refrigerated apple spread

Ingredients:

- 2 Tablespoons unflavored gelatin powder
- 1-quart bottle unsweetened apple juice
- 2 Tablespoons bottled lemon juice
- 2 Tablespoons liquid low-calorie sweetener
- Food coloring, if desired

Directions:

a) In a saucepan, soften the gelatin in the apple and lemon juices. To dissolve gelatin, bring to a full rolling boil and boil 2 minutes. Remove from heat. Stir in sweetener and food coloring, if desired.

b) Fill jars, leaving 1/4-inch headspace. Wipe rims of jars with a dampened clean paper towel. Adjust lids. Do not process or freeze.

c) Store in refrigerator and use within 4 weeks.

28. Refrigerator grape spread

Ingredients:

- 2 Tablespoons unflavored gelatin powder
- 1 bottle (24 oz.) unsweetened grape juice
- 2 Tablespoons bottled lemon juice
- 2 Tablespoons liquid low-calorie sweetener

Directions:

a) In a saucepan, soften the gelatin in the grape and lemon juices. Bring to a full rolling boil to dissolve gelatin. Boil 1 minute and remove from heat. Stir in sweetener.

b) Fill hot jars quickly, leaving 1/4-inch headspace. Wipe rims of jars with a dampened clean paper towel.

c) Adjust lids. Do not process or freeze.

d) Store in refrigerator and use within 4 weeks.

29. Apple Jelly without Added Pectin

Ingredients:

- 4 cups apple juice
- 2 tablespoons strained lemon juice, if desired
- 3 cups sugar

Directions:

a) To prepare juice. Use a proportion of one-fourth under-ripe apples to three-fourths fully ripe tart fruit.

b) Sort, wash and remove stem and blossom ends; do not pare or core. Cut apples into small pieces. Add water, cover, and bring to boil on high heat. Reduce heat and simmer for 20 to 25 minutes or until apples are soft. Extract juice.

c) To make jelly. Measure apple juice into a kettle. Add lemon juice and sugar and stir well. Boil over high heat to 8 °F above the boiling point of water, or until jelly mixture falls in a sheet from a spoon.

d) Remove from heat; skim off foam quickly. Pour jelly immediately into hot, sterile canning jars to $\frac{1}{4}$ inch from top. Seal and process 5 minutes in a boiling water bath.

30. Apple Marmalade without Added Pectin

Ingredients:

- 8 cups thinly sliced apples
- 1 orange
- 1½ cups water
- 5 cups sugar
- 2 tablespoons lemon juice

Directions:

a) To prepare fruit. Select tart apples. Wash, pare, quarter, and core the apples. Slice thin. Quarter the orange, remove any seeds, and slice very thin.

b) To make marmalade. Heat water and sugar until sugar is dissolved. Add the lemon juice and fruit. Boil rapidly, stirring constantly, to 9 °F above the boiling point of water, or until the mixture thickens. Remove from heat; skim.

c) Pour immediately into hot, sterile canning jars to ½ inch from the top. Seal. Process 5 minutes in boiling water bath.

31. Blackberry Jelly without Added Pectin

Ingredients:

- 8 cups blackberry juice
- 6 cups sugar

Directions:

a) To prepare juice. Select a proportion of one-fourth under-ripe berries to three-fourths ripe fruit. Sort and wash; remove any stems or caps. Crush berries, add water, cover, and bring to boil on high heat. Reduce heat and simmer for 5 minutes. Extract juice.

b) To make jelly. Measure juice into a kettle. Add sugar and stir well. Boil over high heat to 8 °F above the boiling point of water or until jelly mixture falls in a sheet from a spoon.

c) Remove from heat; skim off foam quickly. Pour jelly immediately into hot, sterile canning jars to $\frac{1}{4}$ inch from top. Seal, and process 5 minutes in a boiling water bath.

32. Cherry Jelly with Powdered Pectin

Ingredients:

- 3 ½ cups cherry juice
- 1 package powdered pectin
- 4 ½ cups sugar

Directions:

a) To prepare juice. Select fully ripe cherries. Sort, wash, and remove stems; do not pit. Crush cherries, add water, cover, bring to boil on high heat. Reduce heat and simmer for 10 minutes. Extract juice.

b) To make jelly. Measure juice into a kettle. Add pectin and stir well. Place on high heat and, stirring constantly, bring quickly to a full rolling boil that cannot be stirred down.

c) Add sugar, continue stirring, and heat again to a full rolling boil. Boil hard for 1 minute.

d) Remove from heat; skim off foam quickly. Pour jelly into hot, sterile canning jars to ¼ inch from the top. Seal, and process 5 minutes in a boiling water bath.

33. Cherry Jam with Powdered Pectin

Ingredients:

- 4 cups ground pitted cherries
- 1 package powdered pectin
- 5 cups sugar

Directions:

a) To prepare fruit. Sort and wash fully ripe cherries; remove stems and pits. Grind cherries or chop fine.

b) To make jam. Measure pre-pared cherries into a kettle. Add pectin and stir well. Place on high heat and, stirring constantly, bring quickly to a full boil with bubbles over the entire surface.

c) Add sugar, continue stirring, and heat again to a full bubbling boil. Boil hard for 1 minute, stirring constantly. Remove from heat; skim.

d) Pour immediately into hot, sterile canning jars to $\frac{1}{4}$ inch from the top. Seal and process 5 minutes in boiling water bath.

34. Fig Jam with Liquid Pectin

Ingredients:

- 4 cups crushed figs (about 3 pounds figs)
- ½ cup lemon juice
- 7 ½ cups sugar
- ½ bottle liquid pectin

Directions:

a) To prepare fruit. Sort and wash fully ripe figs; remove stem ends. Crush or grind fruit.

b) To make jam. Place crushed figs and lemon juice into a kettle. Add sugar and stir well. Place on high heat and, stirring constantly, bring quickly to a full boil with bubbles over the entire surface. Boil hard for 1 minute, stirring constantly.

c) Remove from heat. Stir in pectin. Skim off foam quickly. Pour immediately into hot, sterile canning jars to ¼ inch from the top. Seal and process 5 minutes in boiling water bath.

35. Grape Jelly with Powdered Pectin

Ingredients:

- 5 cups grape juice
- 1 package powdered pectin
- 7 cups sugar

Directions:

a) To prepare juice. Sort, wash, and remove stems from fully ripe grapes. Crush grapes, add water, cover, and bring to boil on high heat. Reduce heat and simmer for 10 minutes. Extract juice.

b) To make jelly. Measure juice into a kettle. Add pectin and stir well. Place on high heat and, stirring constantly, bring quickly to a full rolling boil that cannot be stirred down.

c) Add sugar, continue stirring, and bring again to a full rolling boil. Boil hard for 1 minute.

d) Remove from heat; skim off foam quickly. Pour jelly immediately into hot, sterile canning jars to $\frac{1}{4}$ inch from the top. Seal and process 5 minutes in a boiling water bath.

Makes 8 or 9 half-pint jars.

36. Mint-Pineapple Jam with Liquid Pectin

Ingredients:

- One 20-oz. can crushed pineapple ¾ cup water
- ¼ cup lemon juice
- 7 ½ cups sugar
- 1 bottle liquid pectin ½ teaspoon mint extract Few drops green coloring

Directions:

a) Place crushed pineapple in a kettle. Add water, lemon juice, and sugar. Stir well.

b) Place on high heat and stirring constantly, bring quickly to a full boil with bubbles over the entire surface. Boil hard for 1 minute, stirring constantly. Remove from heat; add pectin, flavor extract, and coloring. Skim.

c) Pour immediately into hot, sterile canning jars to ¼ inch from the top. Seal and process 5 minutes in boiling water bath.

Makes 9 or 10 half-pint jars.

37. Mixed Fruit Jelly with Liquid Pectin

Ingredients:

- 2 cups cranberry juice
- 2 cups quince juice
- 1 cup apple juice
- 7 ½ cups sugar
- ½ bottle liquid pectin

Directions:

a) To prepare fruit. Sort and wash fully ripe cranberries. Add water, cover, and bring to a boil on high heat. Reduce heat and simmer for 20 minutes. Extract juice.

b) Sort and wash quince. Remove stem and blossom ends; do not pare or core. Slice very thin or cut into small pieces. Add water, cover, and bring to a boil on high heat. Reduce heat and simmer for 25 minutes. Extract juice.

c) Sort and wash apples. Remove stem and blossom ends; do not pare or core. Cut into small pieces. Add water, cover, and bring to a boil on high heat. Reduce heat and simmer 20 minutes. Extract juice.

d) To make jelly. Measure juices into a kettle. Stir in sugar. Place on high heat and, stirring constantly, bring quickly to a full, rolling boil that cannot be stirred down.

e) Add pectin and return to a full, rolling boil. Boil hard for 1 minute.

f) Remove from heat; skim off foam quickly. Pour jelly immediately into hot, sterile canning jars to $\frac{1}{4}$ inch from the top. Seal, and process 5 minutes in a boiling water bath.

Makes nine or ten 8-ounce jars.

38. Orange Jelly

Ingredients:

- 3 ¼ cups sugar
- 1 cup water
- 3 tablespoons lemon juice ½ bottle liquid pectin
- One 6-ounce can (¾ cup) frozen concentrated orange juice

Directions:

a) Stir the sugar into the water. Place on high heat and, stirring constantly, bring quickly to a full, rolling boil that cannot be stirred down.

b) Add lemon juice. Boil hard for 1 minute.

c) Remove from heat. Stir in pectin. Add thawed concentrated orange juice and mix well.

d) Pour jelly immediately into hot, sterile canning jars to ¼ inch from the top. Seal and process 5 minutes in a boiling water bath.

Makes 4 or 5 half-pint jars.

39. Spiced Orange Jelly

Ingredients:

- 2 cups orange juice
- 1/3 cup lemon juice
- 2/3 cup water
- 1 package powdered pectin
- 2 tablespoons orange peel, chopped
- 1 teaspoon whole allspice
- $\frac{1}{2}$ teaspoon whole cloves
- 4 sticks cinnamon, 2 inches long
- 3 $\frac{1}{2}$ cups sugar

Directions:

a) Mix orange juice, lemon juice, and water in a large saucepan.

b) Stir in pectin.

c) Place orange peel, allspice, cloves, and cinnamon sticks loosely in a clean white cloth, tie with a string, and add fruit mixture.

d) Place on high heat and, stirring constantly, bring quickly to a full, rolling boil that cannot be stirred down.

e) Add sugar, continue stirring, and heat again to a full, rolling boil. Boil hard for 1 minute.

f) Remove from heat. Remove spice bag and skim off foam quickly. Pour jelly immediately into hot, sterile canning jars to $\frac{1}{4}$ inch from top. Seal, and process 5 minutes in a boiling water bath.

Makes 4 half-pint jars.

40. Orange Marmalade

Ingredients:

- ¾ cup grapefruit peel (½ grapefruit)
- ¾ cup orange peel (1 orange)
- 13/ cup lemon peel (1 lemon)
- 1-quart cold water
- Pulp of 1 grapefruit
- Pulp of 4 medium-sized oranges
- 2 cups lemon juice
- 2 cups boiling water
- 3 cups sugar

Directions:

a) To prepare fruit. Wash and peel fruit. Cut peel into thin strips. Add cold water and simmer in a covered pan until tender (about 30 minutes). Drain.

b) Remove seeds and membrane from peeled fruit. Cut fruit into small pieces.

c) To make marmalade. Add boiling water to peel and fruit. Add sugar and boil rapidly to 9 °F above the boiling point of water (about 20 minutes), stirring frequently. Remove from heat; skim.

d) Pour immediately into hot, sterile canning jars to $\frac{1}{4}$ inch from the top. Seal and process 5 minutes in boiling water bath.

Makes 3 or 4 half-pint jars.

41. Apricot-Orange Conserve

Ingredients:

- 3 ½ cups chopped drained apricots
- 1 ½ cups orange juice
- Peel of ½ orange, shredded
- 2 tablespoons lemon juice
- 3 ¼ cups sugar
- ½ cup chopped nuts

Directions:

a) To prepare dried apricots. Cook apricots uncovered in 3 cups water until tender (about 20 minutes); drain and chop.

b) To make conserve. Combine all ingredients except nuts. Cook to 9 °F above the boiling point of water or until thick, stirring constantly. Add nuts; stir well. Remove from heat; skim.

c) Pour immediately into hot, sterile canning jars to ¼ inch from the top. Seal, and process 5 minutes in boiling water bath.

Makes about 5 half-pint jars.

42. Peach Jam with Powdered Pectin

Ingredients:

- 3 ¾ cups crushed peaches
- ½ cup lemon juice
- 1 package powdered pectin
- 5 cups sugar

Directions:

a) To prepare fruit. Sort and wash fully ripe peaches. Remove stems, skins, and pits. Crush peaches.

b) To make jam. Measure crushed peaches into a kettle. Add lemon juice and pectin; stir well. Place on high heat and, stir-ring constantly, bring quickly to a full boil with bubbles over the entire surface.

c) Add sugar, continue stirring, and heat again to a full, bubbling boil. Boil hard for 1 minute, stirring constantly. Remove from heat; skim.

d) Pour immediately into hot, sterile canning jars to ¼ inch from the top. Seal, and process 5 minutes in boiling water bath.

Makes about 6 half-pint jars.

43. Spiced Blueberry-Peach Jam

Ingredients:

- 4 cups chopped or ground peaches
- 4 cups blueberries
- 2 tablespoons lemon juice
- $\frac{1}{2}$ cup water
- 5 $\frac{1}{2}$ cups sugar
- $\frac{1}{2}$ teaspoon salt
- 1 stick cinnamon
- $\frac{1}{2}$ teaspoon whole cloves
- $\frac{1}{4}$ teaspoon whole allspice

Directions:

a) To prepare fruit. Sort and wash fully ripe peaches; peel and remove pits. Chop or grind peaches.

b) Sort, wash, and remove any stems from fresh blueberries.

c) Thaw frozen berries.

d) To make jam. Measure fruits into a kettle; add lemon juice and water. Cover, bring to a boil, and simmer for 10 minutes, stirring occasionally.

e) Add sugar and salt; stir well. Add spices tied in cheesecloth. Boil rapidly, stirring constantly, to 9 °F above the boiling point of water, or until the mixture thickens.

f) Pour immediately into hot, sterile canning jars to $\frac{1}{4}$ inch from the top. Seal, and process 5 minutes in boiling water bath.

Makes 6 or 7 half-pint jars.

44. Peach-Orange Marmalade

Ingredients:

- 5 cups chopped or ground peaches
- 1 cup chopped or ground oranges

Directions:

a) Peel of 1 orange, shredded 2 tablespoons lemon juice 6 cups sugar

b) To prepare fruit. Sort and wash fully ripe peaches. Chop or grind the peaches.

c) Remove peel, white portion, and seeds from oranges.

d) Chop or grind the pulp.

e) To make marmalade. Measure the prepared fruit into a kettle. Add remaining ingredients and stir well. Boil rapidly, stirring constantly to 9 °F above the boiling point of water, or until the mixture thickens. Remove from heat; skim.

f) Pour immediately into hot, sterile canning jars to $\frac{1}{4}$ inch from the top. Seal, and process 5 minutes in boiling water bath.

Makes 6 or 7 half-pint jars.

45. Pineapple Jam with Liquid Pectin

Ingredients:

- One 20-ounce can crushed pineapple
- 3 tablespoons lemon juice
- 3 ¼ cups sugar
- ½ bottle liquid pectin

Directions:

a) Combine pineapple and lemon juice in a kettle. Add sugar and stir well. Place on high heat and, stir-ring constantly, bring quickly to a full boil with bubbles over the entire surface.

b) Boil hard for 1 minute, stirring constantly.

c) Remove from heat; stir in pectin. Skim.

d) Let stand for 5 minutes.

e) Pour immediately into hot, sterile canning jars to ¼ inch from the top.

f) Seal, and process 5 minutes in boiling water bath.

Makes 4 or 5 half-pint jars.

46. Plum Jelly with Liquid Pectin

Ingredients:

- 4 cups plum juice
- 7 ½ cups sugar
- ½ bottle liquid pectin

Directions:

a) To prepare juice. Sort and wash fully ripe plums and cut in pieces; do not peel or pit. Crush fruit, add water, cover, and bring to boil over high heat. Reduce heat and simmer for 10 minutes. Extract juice.

b) To make jelly. Measure juice into a kettle. Stir in sugar. Place on high heat and, stirring constantly, bring quickly to a full, rolling boil that cannot be stirred down.

c) Add pectin; bring again to full, rolling boil. Boil hard 1 minute.

d) Remove from heat; skim off foam quickly. Pour jelly immediately into hot, sterile canning jars to ¼ inch from the top. Seal and process 5 minutes in a boiling water bath.

Makes 7 or 8 half-pint jars.

47. Quince Jelly without Added Pectin

Ingredients:

- 3 ¾ cups quince juice
- 1/3 cup lemon juice
- 3 cups sugar

Directions:

a) To prepare juice. Select a proportion of about one-fourth under-ripe quince and three-fourths fully ripe fruit. Sort, wash, and remove stems and blossom ends; do not pare or core. Slice quince very thin or cut into small pieces.

b) Add water, cover, and bring to boil on high heat. Reduce heat and simmer for 25 minutes. Extract juice.

c) To make jelly. Measure quince juice into a kettle. Add lemon juice and sugar. Stir well. Boil over high heat to 8 °F above the boiling point of water, or until jelly mixture forms a sheet from a spoon.

d) Remove from heat; skim off foam quickly. Pour jelly into hot, sterile canning jars to ¼ inch from the top. Seal, and process 5 minutes in a boiling water bath.

e) Makes about four 8-ounce jars.

48. Strawberry Jam with Powdered Pectin

Ingredients:

- 5 ½ cups crushed strawberries
- 1 package powdered pectin
- 8 cups sugar

Directions:

a) To prepare fruit. Sort and wash fully ripe strawberries; remove stems and caps. Crush berries.

b) To make jam. Measure crushed strawberries into a kettle. Add pectin and stir well. Place on high heat and, stirring constantly, bring quickly to a full boil with bubbles over the entire surface.

c) Add sugar, continue stirring, and heat again to a full, bubbling boil. Boil hard for 1 minute, stirring constantly. Remove from heat; skim.

d) Pour immediately into hot, sterile canning jars to ¼ inch from the top. Seal, and process 5 minutes in boiling water bath.

e) Makes 9 or 10 half-pint jars.

49. Tutti-Frutti Jam

Ingredients:

- 3 cups chopped or ground pears
- 1 large orange
- $\frac{3}{4}$ cup drained crushed pineapple
- $\frac{1}{4}$ cup chopped maraschino cherries
- $\frac{1}{4}$ cup lemon juice
- 1 package powdered pectin
- 5 cups sugar

Directions:

a) To prepare fruit. Sort and wash ripe pears; pare and core. Chop or grind the pears. Peel orange, remove seeds, and chop or grind pulp.

b) To make jam. Measure chopped pears into a kettle. Add orange, pineapple, cherries, and lemon juice. Stir in pectin.

c) Place on high heat and, stirring constantly, bring quickly to a full boil with bubbles over the entire surface.

d) Add sugar, continue stirring, and heat again to a full bubbling boil. Boil hard for 1 minute, stirring constantly. Remove from heat; skim.

e) Pour immediately into hot, sterile canning jars to $\frac{1}{4}$ inch from the top. Seal, and process 5 minutes in boiling water bath.

Makes 6 or 7 half-pint jars.

FRUIT AND FRUIT PRODUCTS

50. Apple butter

Ingredients:

- 8 lbs. apples
- 2 cups cider
- 2 cups vinegar
- 2-1/4 cups white sugar
- 2-1/4 cups packed brown sugar
- 2 Tablespoons ground cinnamon
- 1 Tablespoon ground cloves

Directions:

a) Wash, remove stems, quarter, and core fruit. Cook slowly in cider and vinegar until soft. Press fruit through a colander, food mill, or strainer. Cook fruit pulp with sugar and spices, stirring frequently.

b) To test for doneness, remove a spoonful and hold it away from steam for 2 minutes. It is done if the butter remains mounded on the spoon. Another way to determine when the butter is cooked adequately is to spoon a small quantity onto a plate. Fill hot into sterile half-pint or pint jars, leaving 1/4-inch headspace. Wipe rims of jars with a dampened clean paper towel.

c) Adjust lids and process.

51. Spiced apple rings

Ingredients:

- 12 lbs. firm tart apples (maximum diameter, 2-1/2 inches)
- 12 cups sugar
- 6 cups water
- 1-1/4 cups white vinegar (5%)
- 3 Tablespoons whole cloves
- 3/4 cup red hot cinnamon candies or
- 8 cinnamon sticks and
- 1 teaspoon red food coloring (optional)

Directions:

a) Wash apples. To prevent discoloration, peel and slice one apple at a time. Immediately cut crosswise into 1/2-inch slices, remove core area with a melon baller, and immerse in ascorbic acid solution.

b) To make flavored syrup, combine sugar, water, vinegar, cloves, cinnamon candies, or cinnamon sticks and food coloring in a 6-qt saucepan. Stir, heat to boil, and simmer 3 minutes.

c) Drain apples, add to hot syrup, and cook 5 minutes. Fill hot jars (preferably wide-mouth) with apple rings and hot flavored syrup, leaving 1/2-inch headspace.

d) Remove air bubbles and adjust headspace if needed. Wipe rims of jars with a dampened clean paper towel.

e) Adjust lids and process.

52. Spiced crab apples

Ingredients:

- 5 lbs. crab apples
- 4-1/2 cups apple cider vinegar (5%)
- 3-3/4 cups water
- 7-1/2 cups sugar
- 4 teaspoons whole cloves
- 4 sticks cinnamon
- Six 1/2-inch cubes of fresh ginger root

Directions:

a) Remove blossom petals and wash apples, but leave stems attached. Puncture the skin of each apple four times with an ice pick or toothpick. Mix vinegar, water, and sugar and bring to a boil.

b) Add spices tied in a spice bag or cheesecloth. Using a blancher basket or sieve, immerse 1/3 of the apples at a time in the boiling vinegar/syrup solution for 2 minutes. Place cooked apples and spice bag in a clean 1- or 2-gallon crock and add hot syrup.

c) Cover and let stand overnight. Remove spice bag, drain syrup into a large saucepan, and reheat to boiling. Fill hot pint jars with apples and hot syrup, leaving 1/2-inch headspace. Remove air bubbles and adjust headspace if needed.

d) Wipe rims of jars with a dampened clean paper towel. Adjust lids and process.

53. Cantaloupe pickles

Ingredients:

- 5 lbs. of 1-inch cantaloupe cubes
- 1 teaspoon crushed red pepper flakes
- 2 one-inch cinnamon sticks
- 2 teaspoons ground cloves
- 1 teaspoon ground ginger
- 4-1/2 cups cider vinegar (5%)
- 2 cups water
- 1-1/2 cups white sugar
- 1-1/2 cups packed light brown sugar
- Yield: About 4 pint jars

Directions:

Day One:

a) Wash cantaloupe and cut into halves; remove seeds. Cut into 1 inch slices and peel. Cut strips of flesh into 1 inch cubes.

b) Weigh out 5 pounds of pieces and place in large glass bowl. Place red pepper flakes, cinnamon sticks, cloves and ginger in a spice bag and tie the ends firmly.

c) Combine vinegar and water in a 4-quart stockpot. Bring to a boil, then turn heat off. Add spice bag to the vinegar-water mixture, and let steep for 5 minutes, stirring occasionally. Pour hot vinegar solution and spice bag over melon pieces in the bowl. Cover with a food-grade plastic lid or wrap and let stand overnight in the refrigerator (about 18 hours).

Day Two:

d) Carefully pour off vinegar solution into a large 8- to 10-quart saucepan and bring to a boil. Add sugar; stir to dissolve. Add cantaloupe and bring back to a boil. Lower heat and simmer until cantaloupe pieces turn translucent (about 1 to 1-1/4 hours). Remove cantaloupe pieces into a medium-sized stockpot, cover and set aside.

e) Bring remaining liquid to a boil and boil an additional 5 minutes. Return cantaloupe to the liquid syrup, and bring back to a boil. With a slotted spoon, fill hot cantaloupe pieces into hot pint jars, leaving 1-inch headspace. Cover with boiling hot syrup, leaving 1/2-inch headspace.

f) Remove air bubbles and adjust headspace if needed. Wipe rims of jars with a dampened clean paper towel. Adjust lids and process.

54. Cranberry orange chutney

Ingredients:

- 24 ounces fresh whole cranberries
- 2 cups chopped white onion
- 2 cups golden raisin
- 1-1/2 cups white sugar
- 1-1/2 cups packed brown sugar
- 2 cups white distilled vinegar (5%)
- 1 cup orange juice
- 4 teaspoons peeled, grated fresh ginger
- 3 sticks cinnamon

Directions:

a) Rinse cranberries well. Combine all ingredients in a large Dutch oven. Bring to a boil over high heat; reduce heat and simmer gently for 15 minutes or until cranberries are tender. Stir often to prevent scorching.

b) Remove cinnamon sticks and discard. Fill the hot chutney into hot half-pint jars, leaving 1/2-inch headspace.

c) Remove air bubbles and adjust headspace if needed. Wipe rims of jars with a dampened clean paper towel. Adjust lids and process.

55. Mango chutney

Ingredients:

- 11 cups or 4 lbs. chopped unripe mango
- 2-1/2 cups chopped yellow onion
- 2-1/2 Tablespoons grated fresh ginger
- 1-1/2 Tablespoons chopped fresh garlic
- 4-1/2 cups sugar
- 3 cups white distilled vinegar (5%)
- 2-1/2 cups golden raisins
- 1-1 teaspoon canning salt
- 4 teaspoons chili powder

Directions:

a) Wash all produce well. Peel, core and chop mangoes into 3/4-inch cubes. Chop mango cubes in food processor, using 6 one-second pulses per food processor batch. (Do not puree or chop too finely.)

b) By hand, peel and dice onion, chop garlic, and grate ginger. Mix sugar and vinegar in an 8- to 10-quart stockpot. Bring to a boil, and boil 5 minutes. Add all other ingredients and bring back to a boil.

c) Reduce heat and simmer 25 minutes, stirring occasionally. Fill hot chutney into hot pint or half-pint jars, leaving 1/2-inch headspace. Remove air bubbles and adjust headspace if needed.

d) Wipe rims of jars with a dampened clean paper towel. Adjust lids and process.

56. Mango sauce

Ingredients:

- 5-1/2 cups or 3-1/4 lbs. mango puree
- 6 Tablespoons honey
- 4 Tablespoons bottled lemon juice
- 3/4 cup sugar
- 2-1/2 teaspoons (7500 milligrams) ascorbic acid
- 1/8 teaspoons ground cinnamon
- 1/8 teaspoons ground nutmeg

Directions:

a) Wash, peel, and separate mango flesh from seed. Chop mango flesh into chunks and purée in blender or food processor until smooth.

b) Combine all ingredients in a 6- to 8-quart Dutch oven or stockpot and heat on medium-high heat, with continuous stirring, until the mixture reaches 200°F.

c) The mixture will sputter as it is being heated, so be sure to wear gloves or oven mitts to avoid burning skin. Fill hot sauce into hot half-pint jars, leaving 1/4-inch headspace.

d) Remove air bubbles and adjust headspace if needed. Wipe rims of jars with a dampened clean paper towel. Adjust lids and process.

57. Mixed fruit cocktail

Ingredients:

- 3 lbs. peaches
- 3 lbs. pears
- 1-1/2 lbs. slightly under-ripe seedless green grape
- 10-oz jar of maraschino cherries
- 3 cups sugar
- 4 cups water

Directions:

a) Stem and wash grapes, and keep in ascorbic acid solution.

b) Dip ripe but firm peaches, a few at a time, in boiling water for 1 to 1-1/2 minutes to loosen skins.

c) Dip in cold water and slip off skins. Cut in half, remove pits, cut into 1/2-inch cubes and keep in solution with grapes. Peel, halve, and core pears.

d) Cut into 1/2-inch cubes, and keep in solution with grapes and peaches.

e) Combine sugar and water in a saucepan and bring to boil. Drain mixed fruit. Add 1/2 cup of hot syrup to each hot jar.

f) Then add a few cherries and gently fill the jar with mixed fruit and more hot syrup, leaving 1/2-inch headspace.

g) Remove air bubbles and adjust headspace if needed. Wipe rims of jars with a dampened clean paper towel.

h) Adjust lids and process.

58. Zucchini-pineapple

Ingredients:

- 4 quarts cubed or shredded zucchini
- 46 oz. canned unsweetened pineapple juice
- 1-1/2 cups bottled lemon juice
- 3 cups sugar

Directions:

a) Peel zucchini and either cut into 1/2-inch cubes or shred. Mix zucchini with other ingredients in a large saucepan and bring to a boil. Simmer 20 minutes.

b) Fill hot jars with hot mixture and cooking liquid, leaving 1/2-inch headspace. Remove air bubbles and adjust head-space if needed. Wipe rims of jars with a dampened clean paper towel. Adjust lids and process.

59. Spicy cranberry salsa

Ingredients:

- 6 cups chopped red onion
- 4 chopped large Serrano peppers
- 1-1/2 cups water
- 1-1/2 cups cider vinegar (5%)
- 1 Tablespoon canning salt
- 1-1/3 cups sugar
- 6 Tablespoons clover honey
- 12 cups (2-3/4 lbs.) rinsed, fresh whole cranberries

Directions:

a) Combine all ingredients except cranberries in a large Dutch oven. Bring to a boil over high heat; reduce heat slightly and boil gently for 5 minutes.

b) Add cranberries, reduce heat slightly and simmer mixture for 20 minutes, stirring occasionally to prevent scorching. Fill the hot mixture into hot pint jars, leaving 1/4-inch headspace. Leave saucepot over low heat while filling jars.

c) Remove air bubbles and adjust headspace if needed. Wipe rims of jars with a dampened clean paper towel. Adjust lids and process.

60. Mango salsa

Ingredients:

- 6 cups diced unripe mango
- 1-1/2 cups diced red bell pepper
- 1/2 cup chopped yellow onion
- 1/2 teaspoons crushed red pepper flakes
- 2 teaspoons chopped garlic
- 2 teaspoons chopped ginger
- 1 cup light brown sugar
- 1-1/4 cups cider vinegar (5%)
- 1/2 cup water

Directions:

a) Wash all produce well. Peel and chop mango into 1/2-inch cubes. Dice bell pepper into 1/2-inch pieces. Chop yellow onions.

b) Combine all ingredients in an 8-quart Dutch oven or stockpot. Bring to a boil over high heat, stirring to dissolve sugar.

c) Reduce to simmering, and simmer 5 minutes. Fill hot solids into hot half-pint jars, leaving 1/2-inch headspace. Cover with hot liquid, leaving 1/2-inch headspace.

d) Remove air bubbles and adjust headspace if needed. Wipe rims of jars with a dampened clean paper towel. Adjust lids and process.

61. Peach apple salsa

Ingredients:

- 6 cups chopped Roma tomatoes
- 2-1/2 cups diced yellow onions
- 2 cups chopped green bell peppers
- 10 cups chopped hard, unripe peaches
- 2 cups chopped Granny Smith apples
- 4 Tablespoons mixed pickling spice
- 1 Tablespoon canning salt
- 2 teaspoons crushed red pepper flakes
- 3-3/4 cups (1-1/4 pounds) packed light brown sugar
- 2-1/4 cups cider vinegar (5%)

Directions:

a) Place pickling spice on a clean, double-layered, 6-inch-square piece of 100% cheese-cloth. Bring corners together and tie with a clean string. (Or use a purchased muslin spice bag).

b) Wash and peel tomatoes (place washed tomatoes in boiling water for 1 minute, immediately place in cold water, and slip off skins).

c) Chop into 1/2-inch pieces. Peel, wash and dice onions into 1/4-inch pieces. Wash, core, and seed bell peppers; chop into 1/4-inch pieces.

d) Combine chopped tomatoes, onions and peppers in an 8- or 10- quart Dutch oven or saucepot. Wash, peel and pit peaches; cut into halves and soak for 10 minutes in an ascorbic acid solution (1500 mg in half gallon water).

e) Wash, peel and core apples; cut into halves and soak for 10 minutes in ascorbic acid solution.

f) Quickly chop peaches and apples into 1/2-inch cubes to prevent browning. Add chopped peaches and apples to the saucepot with the vegetables. Add the pickling spice bag to the saucepot; stir in the salt, red pepper flakes, brown sugar and vinegar.

g) Bring to boiling, stirring gently to mix ingredients. Reduce heat and simmer 30 minutes, stirring occasionally. Remove spice bag from pan and discard. With a slotted spoon, fill salsa solids into hot pint jars, leaving 1-1/4-inch head-space (about 3/4 pound solids in each jar).

h) Cover with cooking liquid, leaving 1/2-inch headspace.

i) Remove air bubbles and adjust headspace if needed. Wipe rims of jars with a dampened clean paper towel. Adjust lids and process.

FERMENTED AND PICKLED VEGETABLES

62. Dill pickles

Ingredients:

- 4 lbs. of 4-inch pickling cucumber
- 2 Tablespoons dill seed or 4 to 5 heads fresh or dry dill wee
- 1/2 cup salt
- 1/4 cup vinegar (5%
- 8 cups water and one or more of the following ingredients:
- 2 cloves garlic (optional)
- 2 dried red peppers (optional)
- 2 teaspoons whole mixed pickling spices

Directions:

a) Wash cucumbers. Cut 1/16-inch slice of blossom end and discard. Leave 1/4-inch of stem attached. Place half of dill and spices on bottom of a clean, suitable container.

b) Add cucumbers, remaining dill, and spices. Dissolve salt in vinegar and water and pour over cucumbers.

c) Add suitable cover and weight. Store where temperature is between 70° and 75°F for about 3 to 4 weeks while fermenting. Temperatures of 55° to 65°F are acceptable, but the fermentation will take 5 to 6 weeks.

d) Avoid temperatures above 80°F, or pickles will become too soft during fermentation. Fermenting pickles cure slowly. Check the container several times a week and promptly remove surface scum or mold. Caution: If the pickles become soft, slimy, or develop a disagreeable odor, discard them.

e) Fully fermented pickles may be stored in the original container for about 4 to 6 months, provided they are refrigerated and surface scum and molds are removed regularly. Canning fully fermented pickles is a better way to store them. To can them, pour the brine into a pan, heat slowly to a boil, and simmer 5 minutes. Filter brine through paper coffee filters to reduce cloudiness, if desired.

f) Fill hot jar with pickles and hot brine, leaving 1/2-inch headspace.

g) Remove air bubbles and adjust headspace if needed. Wipe rims of jars with a dampened clean paper towel.

h) Adjust lids and process.

63. Sauerkraut

Ingredients:

- 25 lbs. cabbage
- 3/4 cup canning or pickling salt

Directions:

a) Work with about 5 pounds of cabbage at a time. Discard outer leaves. Rinse heads under cold running water and drain. Cut heads in quarters and remove cores. Shred or slice to a thickness of a quarter.

b) Put cabbage in a suitable fermentation container and add 3 tablespoons of salt. Mix thoroughly, using clean hands. Pack firmly until salt draws juices from cabbage.

c) Repeat shredding, salting, and packing until all cabbage is in the container. Be sure it is deep enough so that its rim is at least 4 or 5 inches above the cabbage. If juice does not cover cabbage, add boiled and cooled brine (1-1/2 tablespoons of salt per quart of water).

d) Add plate and weights; cover container with a clean bath towel. Store at 70° to 75°F while fermenting. At temperatures between 70° and 75°F, kraut will be fully fermented in about 3 to 4 weeks; at 60° to 65°F, fermentation may take 5 to 6 weeks. At temperatures lower than 60°F, kraut may not ferment. Above 75°F, kraut may become soft.

e) If you weigh the cabbage down with a brine-filled bag, do not disturb the crock until normal fermentation is completed (when bubbling ceases). If you use jars as weight, you will have to check the kraut two to three times each week and remove scum if it forms. Fully fermented kraut may be kept tightly covered in the refrigerator for several months.

f) Remove air bubbles and adjust headspace if needed. Wipe rims of jars with a dampened clean paper towel. Adjust lids and process.

64. Bread-and-butter pickles

Ingredients:

- 6 lbs. of 4- to 5-inch pickling cucumbers
- 8 cups thinly sliced onions
- 1/2 cup canning or pickling salt
- 4 cups vinegar (5%)
- 4-1/2 cups sugar
- 2 Tablespoons mustard seed
- 1-1/2 Tablespoons celery seed
- 1 Tablespoon ground turmeric
- 1 cup pickling lime

Directions:

a) Wash cucumbers. Cut 1/16-inch of blossom end and discard. Cut into 3/16-inch slices. Combine cucumbers and onions in a large bowl. Add salt. Cover with 2 inches crushed or cubed ice. Refrigerate 3 to 4 hours, adding more ice as needed.

b) Combine remaining ingredients in a large pot. Boil 10 minutes. Drain and add cucumbers and onions and slowly reheat to boiling. Fill hot pint jars with slices and cooking syrup, leaving 1/2-inch headspace. Remove air bubbles and adjust headspace if needed. Wipe rims of jars with a dampened clean paper towel.

c) Adjust lids and process.

65. Fresh-pack dill pickles

Ingredients:

- 8 lbs. of 3- to 5-inch pickling cucumbers
- 2 gallons water
- 1-1/4 cups canning or pickling salt
- 1-1/2 quarts vinegar (5%)
- 1/4 cup sugar
- 2 quarts water
- 2 Tablespoons whole mixed pickling spice
- about 3 Tablespoons whole mustard seed
- about 14 heads of fresh dill (1-1/2 heads per pint jar) or
- 4-1/2 Tablespoons dill seed (1-1/2 teaspoons per pint jar)

Directions:

a) Wash cucumbers. Cut 1/16-inch slice of blossom end and discard, but leave 1/4-inch of stem attached. Dissolve 3/4 cup salt in 2 gallons water. Pour over cucumbers and let stand 12 hours. Drain.

b) Combine vinegar, 1/2 cup salt, sugar, and 2 quarts water. Add mixed pickling spices tied in a clean white cloth. Heat to boiling. Fill hot jars with cucumbers.

c) Add 1 teaspoon mustard seed and 1-1/2 heads fresh dill per pint. Cover with boiling pickling solution, leaving 1/2-inch head-space. Remove air bubbles and adjust headspace if needed. Wipe rims of jars with a dampened clean paper towel.

d) Adjust lids and process.

66. Sweet gherkin pickles

Ingredients:

- 7 lbs. cucumbers (1-1/2 inch or less)
- 1/2 cup canning or pickling salt
- 8 cups sugar
- 6 cups vinegar (5%)
- 3/4 teaspoons turmeric
- 2 teaspoons celery seeds
- 2 teaspoons whole mixed pickling spice
- 2 cinnamon sticks
- 1/2 teaspoons fennel (optional)
- 2 teaspoons vanilla (optional)

Directions:

a) Wash cucumbers. Cut 1/16-inch slice of blossom end and discard, but leave 1/4-inch of stem attached.

b) Place cucumbers in large container and cover with boiling water. Six to 8 hours later, and again on the second day, drain and cover with 6 quarts of fresh boiling water containing 1/4-cup salt. On the third day, drain and prick cucumbers with a table fork.

c) Combine and bring to a boil 3 cups vinegar, 3 cups sugar, turmeric, and spices. Pour over cucumbers. Six to 8 hours later, drain and save the pickling syrup. Add another 2 cups each of sugar and vinegar and reheat to boil. Pour over pickles.

d) On the fourth day, drain and save syrup. Add another 2 cups sugar and 1 cup vinegar. Heat to boiling and pour over pickles. Drain and save pickling syrup 6 to 8 hours later. Add 1 cup sugar and 2 teaspoons vanilla and heat to boiling.

e) Fill hot sterile pint jars with pickles and cover with hot syrup, leaving 1/2-inch headspace.

f) Remove air bubbles and adjust headspace if needed. Wipe rims of jars with a dampened clean paper towel.

g) Adjust lids and process.

67. 14-Day sweet pickles

Ingredients:

- 4 lbs. of 2- to 5-inch pickling cucumbers
- 3/4 cup canning or pickling salt
- 2 teaspoons celery seed
- 2 Tablespoons mixed pickling spices
- 5-1/2 cups sugar
- 4 cups vinegar (5%)

Directions:

a) Wash cucumbers. Cut 1/16-inch slice of blossom end and discard, but leave 1/4-inch of stem attached. Place whole cucumbers in suitable 1-gallon container.

b) Add 1/4 cup canning or pickling salt to 2 quarts water and bring to a boil. Pour over cucumbers. Add suitable cover and weight.

c) Place clean towel over container and keep the temperature at about 70°F. On the third and fifth days, drain salt water and discard. Rinse cucumbers and return cucumbers to container. Add 1/4 cup salt to 2 quarts fresh water and boil. Pour over cucumbers.

d) Replace cover and weight, and re-cover with clean towel. On the seventh day, drain salt water and discard. Rinse cucumbers, cover, and weight.

68. Quick sweet pickles

Ingredients:

- 8 lbs. of 3- to 4-inch pickling cucumbers
- 1/3 cup canning or pickling salt
- 4-1/2 cups sugar
- 3-1/2 cups vinegar (5%)
- 2 teaspoons celery seed
- 1 Tablespoon whole allspice
- 2 Tablespoons mustard seed
- 1 cup pickling lime (optional)

Directions:

a) Wash cucumbers. Cut 1/16-inch of blossom end and discard, but leave 1/4 inch of stem attached. Slice or cut in strips, if desired. Place in bowl and sprinkle with 1/3 cup salt. Cover with 2 inches of crushed or cubed ice.

b) Refrigerate 3 to 4 hours. Add more ice as needed. Drain well.

c) Combine sugar, vinegar, celery seed, allspice, and mustard seed in 6-quart kettle. Heat to boiling.

d) Hot pack—Add cucumbers and heat slowly until vinegar solution returns to boil. Stir occasionally to make sure mixture heats evenly. Fill sterile jars, leaving 1/2-inch headspace.

e) Raw pack—Fill hot jars, leaving 1/2-inch headspace. Add hot pickling syrup, leaving 1/2-inch headspace.

f) Remove air bubbles and adjust headspace if needed. Wipe rims of jars with a dampened clean paper towel.

g) Adjust lids and process.

69. Pickled asparagus

Ingredients:

- 10 lbs. asparagus
- 6 large garlic cloves
- 4-1/2 cups water
- 4-1/2 cups white distilled vinegar (5%)
- 6 small hot peppers (optional)
- 1/2 cup canning salt
- 3 teaspoons dill seed

Directions:

a) Wash asparagus well, but gently, under running water. Cut stems from the bottom to leave spears with tips that it into the canning jar, leaving a little more than 1/2-inch headspace. Peel and wash garlic cloves.

b) Place a garlic clove at the bottom of each jar, and tightly pack asparagus into hot jars with the blunt ends down. In an 8-quart saucepot, combine water, vinegar, hot peppers (optional), salt and dill seed.

c) Bring to a boil. Place one hot pepper (if used) in each jar over asparagus spears. Pour boiling hot pickling brine over spears, leaving 1/2-inch headspace.

d) Remove air bubbles and adjust headspace if needed. Wipe rims of jars with a dampened clean paper towel.

e) Adjust lids and process.

70. Pickled dilled beans

Ingredients:

- 4 lbs. fresh tender green or yellow beans
- 8 to 16 heads fresh dill
- 8 cloves garlic (optional)
- 1/2 cup canning or pickling salt
- 4 cups white vinegar (5%)
- 4 cups water
- 1 teaspoon hot red pepper lakes (optional)

Directions:

a) Wash and trim ends from beans and cut to 4-inch lengths. In each hot sterile pint jar, place 1 to 2 dill heads and, if desired, 1 clove of garlic. Place whole beans upright in jars, leaving 1/2-inch headspace.

b) Trim beans to ensure proper it, if necessary. Combine salt, vinegar, water, and pepper lakes (if desired). Bring to a boil. Add hot solution to beans, leaving 1/2-inch headspace.

c) Remove air bubbles and adjust headspace if needed. Wipe rims of jars with a dampened clean paper towel.

d) Adjust lids and process.

71. Pickled three-bean salad

Ingredients:

- 1-1/2 cups blanched green/yellow beans
- 1-1/2 cups canned, drained, red kidney beans
- 1 cup canned, drained garbanzo beans
- 1/2 cup peeled and thinly sliced onion
- 1/2 cup trimmed and thinly sliced celery
- 1/2 cup sliced green peppers
- 1/2 cup white vinegar (5%)
- 1/4 cup bottled lemon juice
- 3/4 cup sugar
- 1/4 cup oil
- 1/2 teaspoons canning or pickling salt
- 1-1/4 cups water

Directions:

a) Wash and snap of ends of fresh beans. Cut or snap into 1- to 2-inch pieces.

b) Blanch 3 minutes and cool immediately. Rinse kidney beans with tap water and drain again. Prepare and measure all other vegetables.

c) Combine vinegar, lemon juice, sugar, and water and bring to a boil. Remove from heat.

d) Add oil and salt and mix well. Add beans, onions, celery, and green pepper to solution and bring to a simmer.

e) Marinate 12 to 14 hours in refrigerator, then heat entire mixture to a boil. Fill hot jars with solids. Add hot liquid, leaving 1/2-inch headspace.

f) Remove air bubbles and adjust headspace if needed. Wipe rims of jars with a dampened clean paper towel.

g) Adjust lids and process.

72. Pickled beets

Ingredients:

- 7 lbs. of 2- to 2-1/2-inch diameter beets
- 4 cups vinegar (5%)
- 1-1/2 teaspoons canning or pickling salt
- 2 cups sugar
- 2 cups water
- 2 cinnamon sticks
- 12 whole cloves
- 4 to 6 onions (2- to 2-1/2-inch diameter),

Directions:

a) Trim of beet tops, leaving 1 inch of stem and roots to prevent bleeding of color.

b) Wash thoroughly. Sort for size. Cover similar sizes together with boiling water and cook until tender (about 25 to 30 minutes). Caution: Drain and discard liquid. Cool beets. Trim of roots and stems and slip of skins. Slice into 1/4-inch slices. Peel and thinly slice onions.

c) Combine vinegar, salt, sugar, and fresh water. Put spices in cheesecloth bag and add to vinegar mixture. Bring to a boil. Add beets and onions. Simmer 5 minutes. Remove spice bag.

d) Fill hot jars with beets and onions, leaving 1/2-inch headspace. Add hot vinegar solution, allowing 1/2-inch headspace.

e) Remove air bubbles and adjust headspace if needed. Wipe rims of jars with a dampened clean paper towel.

f) Adjust lids and process.

73. Pickled carrots

Ingredients:

- 2-3/4 lbs. peeled carrots
- 5-1/2 cups white vinegar (5%)
- 1 cup water
- 2 cups sugar
- 2 teaspoons canning salt
- 8 teaspoons mustard seed
- 4 teaspoons celery seed

Directions:

a) Wash and peel carrots. Cut into rounds that are approximately 1/2-inch thick.

b) Combine vinegar, water, sugar and canning salt in an 8-quart Dutch oven or stockpot. Bring to a boil and boil 3 minutes. Add carrots and bring back to a boil. Then reduce heat to a simmer and heat until half-cooked (about 10 minutes).

c) Meanwhile, place 2 teaspoons mustard seed and 1 tea-spoon celery seed into each empty hot pint jar. Fill jars with hot carrots, leaving 1-inch headspace. Fill with hot pickling liquid, leaving 1/2-inch headspace.

d) Remove air bubbles and adjust headspace if needed. Wipe rims of jars with a dampened clean paper towel.

e) Adjust lids and process.

74. Pickled cauliflower/Brussels

Ingredients:

- 12 cups of 1- to 2-inch cauliflower flowerets or small Brussels sprouts
- 4 cups white vinegar (5%)
- 2 cups sugar
- 2 cups thinly sliced onions
- 1 cup diced sweet red peppers
- 2 Tablespoons mustard seed
- 1 Tablespoon celery seed
- 1 teaspoon turmeric
- 1 teaspoon hot red pepper lakes

Directions:

a) Wash cauliflower flowerets or Brussels sprouts (remove stems and blemished outer leaves) and boil in salt water (4 teaspoons canning salt per gallon of water) for 3 minutes for cauliflower and 4 minutes for Brussels sprouts. Drain and cool.

b) Combine vinegar, sugar, onion, diced red pepper, and spices in large saucepan. Bring to a boil and simmer 5 minutes.

Distribute onion and diced pepper among jars. Fill hot jars with pieces and pickling solution, leaving 1/2-inch headspace.

c) Remove air bubbles and adjust headspace if needed. Wipe rims of jars with a dampened clean paper towel.

d) Adjust lids and process.

75. Chayote and jicama slaw

Ingredients:

- 4 cups julienned jicama
- 4 cups julienned chayote
- 2 cups chopped red bell pepper
- 2 chopped hot peppers
- 2-1/2 cups water
- 2-1/2 cups cider vinegar (5%)
- 1/2 cup white sugar
- 3-1/2 teaspoons canning salt
- 1 teaspoon celery seed (optional)

Directions:

a) Caution: Wear plastic or rubber gloves and do not touch your face while handling or cutting hot peppers. If you do not wear gloves, wash hands thoroughly with soap and water before touching your face or eyes.

b) Wash, peel and thinly julienne jicama and chayote, discarding the seed of the chayote. In an 8-quart Dutch oven or stockpot, combine all ingredients except chayote. Bring to a boil and boil for 5 minutes.

c) Reduce heat to simmering and add chayote. Bring back to a boil and then turn heat of. Fill hot solids into hot half-pint jars, leaving 1/2-inch headspace.

d) Cover with boiling cooking liquid, leaving 1/2-inch headspace.

e) Remove air bubbles and adjust headspace if needed. Wipe rims of jars with a dampened clean paper towel.

f) Adjust lids and process.

76. Bread-and-butter pickled jicama

Ingredients:

- 14 cups cubed jicama
- 3 cups thinly sliced onion
- 1 cup chopped red bell pepper
- 4 cups white vinegar (5%)
- 4-1/2 cups sugar
- 2 Tablespoons mustard seed
- 1 Tablespoon celery seed
- 1 teaspoon ground turmeric

Directions:

a) Combine vinegar, sugar and spices in a 12-quart Dutch oven or large saucepot. Stir and bring to a boil. Stir in prepared jicama, onion slices, and red bell pepper. Return to a boil, reduce heat and simmer 5 minutes. Stir occasionally.

b) Fill hot solids into hot pint jars, leaving 1/2-inch headspace. Cover with boiling cooking liquid, leaving 1/2-inch headspace.

c) Remove air bubbles and adjust headspace if needed. Wipe rims of jars with a dampened clean paper towel.

d) Adjust lids and process.

77. Marinated whole mushrooms

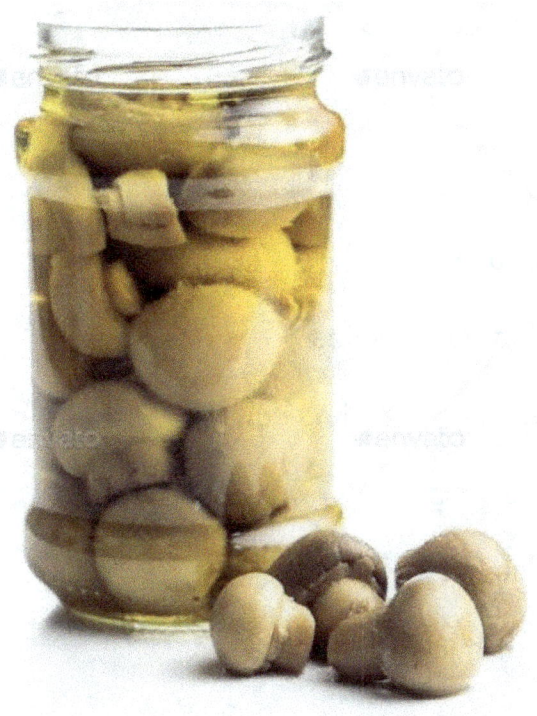

Ingredients:

- 7 lbs. small whole mushrooms
- 1/2 cup bottled lemon juice
- 2 cups olive or salad oil
- 2-1/2 cups white vinegar (5%)
- 1 Tablespoon oregano leaves
- 1 Tablespoon dried basil leaves
- 1 Tablespoon canning or pickling salt
- 1/2 cup chopped onions
- 1/4 cup diced pimiento
- 2 cloves garlic, cut in quarters
- 25 black peppercorns

Directions:

a) Select very fresh unopened mushrooms with caps less than 1-1/4 inch in diameter. Wash. Cut stems, leaving 1/4 inch attached to cap. Add lemon juice and water to cover. Bring to boil. Simmer 5 minutes. Drain mushrooms.

b) Mix olive oil, vinegar, oregano, basil, and salt in a saucepan. Stir in onions and pimiento and heat to boiling.

c) Place 1/4 garlic clove and 2-3 peppercorns in a half-pint jar. Fill hot jars with mushrooms and hot, well-mixed oil/vinegar solution, leaving 1/2-inch headspace.

d) Remove air bubbles and adjust headspace if needed. Wipe rims of jars with a dampened clean paper towel.

e) Adjust lids and process.

78. Pickled dilled okra

Ingredients:

- 7 lbs. small okra pods
- 6 small hot peppers
- 4 teaspoons dill seed
- 8 to 9 garlic cloves
- 2/3 cup canning or pickling salt
- 6 cups water
- 6 cups vinegar (5%)

Directions:

a) Wash and trim okra. Fill hot jars firmly with whole okra, leaving 1/2-inch headspace. Place 1 garlic clove in each jar.

b) Combine salt, hot peppers, dill seed, water, and vinegar in large saucepan and bring to a boil. Pour hot pickling solution over okra, leaving 1/2-inch headspace.

c) Remove air bubbles and adjust headspace if needed. Wipe rims of jars with a dampened clean paper towel.

d) Adjust lids and process.

79. Pickled pearl onions

Ingredients:

- 8 cups peeled white pearl onions
- 5-1/2 cups white vinegar (5%)
- 1 cup water
- 2 teaspoons canning salt
- 2 cups sugar
- 8 teaspoons mustard seed
- 4 teaspoons celery seed

Directions:

a) To peel onions, place a few at a time in a wire-mesh basket or strainer, dip in boiling water for 30 seconds, then remove and place in cold water for 30 seconds. Cut a 1/16th-inch slice from the root end, and then remove the peel and cut 1/16th-inch from the other end of the onion.

b) Combine vinegar, water, salt and sugar in an 8-quart Dutch oven or stockpot. Bring to a boil and boil 3 minutes.

c) Add peeled onions and bring back to a boil. Reduce heat to a simmer and heat until half-cooked (about 5 minutes).

d) Meanwhile, place 2 teaspoons mustard seed and 1 teaspoon celery seed into each empty hot pint jar. Fill with hot onions, leaving 1-inch headspace. Fill with hot pickling liquid, leaving 1/2-inch headspace.

e) Remove air bubbles and adjust headspace if needed. Wipe rims of jars with a dampened clean paper towel.

f) Adjust lids and process.

80. Marinated peppers

Ingredients:

- Bell, Hungarian, banana, or jalapeño
- 4 lbs. firm peppers
- 1 cup bottled lemon juice
- 2 cups white vinegar (5%)
- 1 Tablespoon oregano leaves
- 1 cup olive or salad oil
- 1/2 cup chopped onions
- 2 cloves garlic, quartered (optional)
- 2 Tablespoons prepared horseradish (optional)

Directions:

a) Select your favorite pepper. Caution: If you select hot peppers, wear plastic or rubber gloves and do not touch your face while handling or cutting hot peppers.

b) Wash, slash two to four slits in each pepper, and blanch in boiling water or blister skins on tough-skinned hot peppers using one of these two methods:

c) Oven or broiler method to blister skins – Place peppers in a hot oven (400°F) or under a broiler for 6 to 8 minutes until skins blister.

d) Range-top method to blister skins – Cover hot burner (either gas or electric) with heavy wire mesh.

e) Place peppers on burner for several minutes until skins blister.

f) After blistering skins, place peppers in a pan and cover with a damp cloth. (This will make peeling the peppers easier.) Cool several minutes; peel of skins. Flatten whole peppers.

g) Mix all remaining ingredients in a saucepan and heat to boiling. Place 1/4 garlic clove (optional) and 1/4 teaspoon salt in each hot half-pint jar or 1/2 teaspoon per pint. Fill hot jars with peppers. Add hot, well-mixed oil/pickling solution over peppers, leaving 1/2-inch headspace.

h) Remove air bubbles and adjust headspace if needed. Wipe rims of jars with a dampened clean paper towel.

i) Adjust lids and process.

81. Pickled bell peppers

Ingredients:

- 7 lbs. firm bell peppers
- 3-1/2 cups sugar
- 3 cups vinegar (5%)
- 3 cups water
- 9 cloves garlic
- 4-1/2 teaspoons canning or pickling salt

Directions:

a) Wash peppers, cut into quarters, remove cores and seeds, and cut away any blemishes. Slice peppers in strips. Boil sugar, vinegar, and water for 1 minute.

b) Add peppers and bring to a boil. Place 1/2 clove of garlic and 1/4 teaspoon salt in each hot sterile half-pint jar; double the amounts for pint jars.

c) Add pepper strips and cover with hot vinegar mixture, leaving 1/2-inch

82. Pickled hot peppers

Ingredients:

- Hungarian, banana, chile, jalapeño
- 4 lbs. hot long red, green, or yellow peppers
- 3 lbs. sweet red and green peppers, mixed
- 5 cups vinegar (5%)
- 1 cup water
- 4 teaspoons canning or pickling salt
- 2 Tablespoons sugar
- 2 cloves garlic

Directions:

a) Caution: Wear plastic or rubber gloves and do not touch your face while handling or cutting hot peppers. If you do not wear gloves, wash hands thoroughly with soap and water before touching your face or eyes.

b) Wash peppers. If small peppers are left whole, slash 2 to 4 slits in each. Quarter large peppers.

c) Blanch in boiling water or blister skins on tough-skinned hot peppers using one of these two methods:

d) Oven or broiler method to blister skins – Place peppers in a hot oven (400°F) or under a broiler for 6 to 8 minutes until skins blister.

e) Range-top method to blister skins – Cover hot burner (either gas or electric) with heavy wire mesh.

f) Place peppers on burner for several minutes until skins blister.

g) After blistering skins, place peppers in a pan and cover with a damp cloth. (This will make peeling the peppers easier.) Cool several minutes; peel of skins. Flatten small peppers. Quarter large peppers. Fill hot jars with peppers, leaving 1/2-inch headspace.

h) Combine and heat other ingredients to boiling and simmer 10 minutes. Remove garlic. Add hot pickling solution over peppers, leaving 1/2-inch headspace.

i) Remove air bubbles and adjust headspace if needed. Wipe rims of jars with a dampened clean paper towel.

j) Adjust lids and process.

83. Pickled jalapeño pepper rings

Ingredients:

- 3 lbs. jalapeño peppers
- 1-1/2 cups pickling lime
- 1-1/2 gallons water
- 7-1/2 cups cider vinegar (5%)
- 1-3/4 cups water
- 2-1/2 Tablespoons canning salt
- 3 Tablespoons celery seed
- 6 Tablespoons mustard seed

Directions:

a) Caution: Wear plastic or rubber gloves and do not touch your face while handling or cutting hot peppers.

b) Wash peppers well and slice into 1/4-inch thick slices. Discard stem end.

c) Mix 1-1/2 cups pickling lime with 1-1/2 gallons water in a stainless steel, glass or food grade plastic container. Avoid inhaling lime dust while mixing the lime-water solution.

d) Soak pepper slices in the lime water, in refrigerator, for 18 hours, stirring occasionally (12 to 24 hours may be used). Drain lime solution from soaked pepper rings.

e) Rinse peppers gently but thoroughly with water. Cover pepper rings with fresh cold water and soak, in refrigerator, 1 hour. Drain water from peppers. Repeat the rinsing, soaking and draining steps two more times. Drain thoroughly at the end.

f) Place 1 tablespoon mustard seed and 1-1/2 teaspoons celery seed in the bottom of each hot pint jar. Pack drained pepper rings into the jars, leaving 1/2-inch headspace. Bring cider vinegar, 1-3/4 cups water and canning salt to a boil over high heat. Ladle boiling hot brine solution over pepper rings in jars, leaving 1/2-inch headspace.

g) Remove air bubbles and adjust headspace if needed. Wipe rims of jars with a dampened clean paper towel.

h) Adjust lids and process.

84. Pickled yellow pepper rings

Ingredients:

- 2-1/2 to 3 lbs. yellow (banana) peppers
- 2 Tablespoons celery seed
- 4 Tablespoons mustard seed
- 5 cups cider vinegar (5%)
- 1-1/4 cups water
- 5 teaspoons canning salt

Directions:

a) Wash peppers well and remove stem end; slice peppers into 1/4-inch thick rings. Place 1/2 tablespoon celery seed and 1 tablespoon mustard seed in the bottom of each empty hot pint jar.

b) Fill pepper rings into jars, leaving 1/2-inch head-space. In a 4-quart Dutch oven or saucepan, combine the cider vinegar, water and salt; heat to boiling. Cover pepper rings with boiling pickling liquid, leaving 1/2-inch headspace.

c) Remove air bubbles and adjust headspace if needed. Wipe rims of jars with a dampened clean paper towel.

d) Adjust lids and process.

85. Pickled sweet green tomatoes

Ingredients:

- 10 to 11 lbs. of green tomatoes
- 2 cups sliced onions
- 1/4 cup canning or pickling salt
- 3 cups brown sugar
- 4 cups vinegar (5%)
- 1 Tablespoon mustard seed
- 1 Tablespoon allspice
- 1 Tablespoon celery seed
- 1 Tablespoon whole cloves

Directions:

a) Wash and slice tomatoes and onions. Place in bowl, sprinkle with 1/4 cup salt, and let stand 4 to 6 hours. Drain. Heat and stir sugar in vinegar until dissolved.

b) Tie mustard seed, allspice, celery seed, and cloves in a spice bag. Add to vinegar with tomatoes and onions. If needed, add minimum water to cover pieces. Bring to boil and simmer 30 minutes, stirring as needed to prevent burning. Tomatoes should be tender and transparent when properly cooked.

c) Remove spice bag. Fill hot jar with solids and cover with hot pickling solution, leaving 1/2-inch headspace.

d) Remove air bubbles and adjust headspace if needed. Wipe rims of jars with a dampened clean paper towel.

e) Adjust lids and process.

86. Pickled mixed vegetables

Ingredients:

- 4 lbs. of 4- to 5-inch pickling cucumbers
- 2 lbs. peeled and quartered small onions
- 4 cups cut celery (1-inch pieces)
- 2 cups peeled and cut carrots (1/2-inch pieces)
- 2 cups cut sweet red peppers (1/2-inch pieces)
- 2 cups cauliflower flowerets
- 5 cups white vinegar (5%)
- 1/4 cup prepared mustard
- 1/2 cup canning or pickling salt
- 3-1/2 cups sugar
- 3 Tablespoons celery seed
- 2 Tablespoons mustard seed
- 1/2 teaspoons whole cloves
- 1/2 teaspoons ground turmeric

Directions:

a) Combine vegetables, cover with 2 inches of cubed or crushed ice, and refrigerate 3 to 4 hours.

b) In 8-quart kettle, combine vinegar and mustard and mix well.

c) Add salt, sugar, celery seed, mustard seed, cloves, turmeric. Bring to a boil. Drain vegetables and add to hot pickling solution.

d) Cover and slowly bring to boil. Drain vegetables but save pickling solution. Fill vegetables in hot sterile pint jars, or hot quarts, leaving 1/2-inch headspace. Add pickling solution, leaving 1/2-inch headspace.

e) Remove air bubbles and adjust headspace if needed. Wipe rims of jars with a dampened clean paper towel.

f) Adjust lids and process.

87. Pickled bread-and-butter zucchini

Ingredients:

- 16 cups fresh zucchini, sliced
- 4 cups onions, thinly sliced
- 1/2 cup canning or pickling salt
- 4 cups white vinegar (5%)
- 2 cups sugar
- 4 Tablespoons mustard seed
- 2 Tablespoons celery seed
- 2 teaspoons ground turmeric

Directions:

a) Cover zucchini and onion slices with 1 inch of water and salt. Let stand 2 hours and drain thoroughly. Combine vinegar, sugar, and spices. Bring to a boil and add zucchini and onions. Simmer 5 minutes and ill hot jars with mixture and pickling solution, leaving 1/2-inch headspace.

b) Remove air bubbles and adjust headspace if needed. Wipe rims of jars with a dampened clean paper towel.

c) Adjust lids and process.

88. Chayote and pear relish

Ingredients:

- 3-1/2 cups peeled, cubed chayote
- 3-1/2 cups peeled, cubed Seckel pears
- 2 cups chopped red bell pepper
- 2 cups chopped yellow bell pepper
- 3 cups chopped onion
- 2 Serrano peppers, chopped
- 2-1/2 cups cider vinegar (5%)
- 1-1/2 cups water
- 1 cup white sugar
- 2 teaspoons canning salt
- 1 teaspoon ground allspice
- 1 teaspoon ground pumpkin pie spice

Directions:

a) Wash, peel and cut chayote and pears into 1/2-inch cubes, discarding cores and seeds. Chop onions and peppers. Combine vinegar, water, sugar, salt and spices in a Dutch oven or large saucepot. Bring to a boil, stirring to dissolve sugar.

b) Add chopped onions and peppers; return to a boil and boil for 2 minutes, stirring occasionally.

c) Add cubed chayote and pears; return to the boiling point and turn off heat. Fill the hot solids into hot pint jars, leaving 1-inch headspace. Cover with boiling cooking liquid, leaving 1/2-inch head-space.

d) Remove air bubbles and adjust headspace if needed. Wipe rims of jars with a dampened clean paper towel.

e) Adjust lids and process.

89. Piccalilli

Ingredients:

- 6 cups chopped green tomatoes
- 1-1/2 cups chopped sweet red peppers
- 1-1/2 cups chopped green peppers
- 2-1/4 cups chopped onions
- 7-1/2 cups chopped cabbage
- 1/2 cup canning or pickling salt
- 3 Tablespoons whole mixed pickling spice
- 4-1/2 cups vinegar (5%)
- 3 cups brown sugar

Directions:

a) Wash, chop, and combine vegetables with 1/2 cup salt. Cover with hot water and let stand 12 hours. Drain and press in a clean white cloth to remove all possible liquid. Tie spices loosely in a spice bag and add to combined vinegar and brown sugar and heat to a boil in a sauce pan.

b) Add vegetables and boil gently 30 minutes or until the volume of the mixture is reduced by one-half. Remove spice bag.

c) Fill hot sterile jars, with hot mixture, leaving 1/2-inch headspace.

d) Remove air bubbles and adjust headspace if needed. Wipe rims of jars with a dampened clean paper towel.

e) Adjust lids and process.

90. Pickle relish

Ingredients:

- 3 quarts chopped cucumbers
- 3 cups each of chopped sweet green and red peppers
- 1 cup chopped onions
- 3/4 cup canning or pickling salt
- 4 cups ice
- 8 cups water
- 2 cups sugar
- 4 teaspoons each of mustard seed, turmeric, whole allspice, and whole cloves
- 6 cups white vinegar (5%)

Directions:

a) Add cucumbers, peppers, onions, salt, and ice to water and let stand 4 hours. Drain and re-cover vegetables with fresh ice water for another hour. Drain again.

b) Combine spices in a spice or cheesecloth bag. Add spices to sugar and vinegar. Heat to boiling and pour mixture over vegetables.

c) Cover and refrigerate 24 hours. Heat mixture to boiling and ill hot into hot jars, leaving 1/2-inch headspace.

d) Remove air bubbles and adjust headspace if needed. Wipe rims of jars with a dampened clean paper towel.

e) Adjust lids and process.

91. Pickled corn relish

Ingredients:

- 10 cups fresh whole kernel corn
- 2-1/2 cups diced sweet red peppers
- 2-1/2 cups diced sweet green peppers
- 2-1/2 cups chopped celery
- 1-1/4 cups diced onions
- 1-3/4 cups sugar
- 5 cups vinegar (5%)
- 2-1/2 Tablespoons canning or pickling salt
- 2-1/2 teaspoons celery seed
- 2-1/2 Tablespoons dry mustard
- 1-1/4 teaspoons turmeric

Directions:

a) Boil ears of corn 5 minutes. Dip in cold water. Cut whole kernels from cob or use six 10-ounce frozen packages of corn.

b) Combine peppers, celery, onions, sugar, vinegar, salt, and celery seed in a saucepan.

c) Bring to boil and simmer 5 minutes, stirring occasionally. Mix mustard and turmeric in 1/2 cup of the simmered mixture. Add this mixture and corn to the hot mixture.

d) Simmer another 5 minutes. If desired, thicken mixture with lour paste (1/4 cup lour blended in 1/4 cup water) and stir frequently. Fill hot jars with hot mixture, leaving 1/2-inch headspace.

e) Remove air bubbles and adjust headspace if needed. Wipe rims of jars with a dampened clean paper towel.

f) Adjust lids and process.

92. Pickled green tomato relish

Ingredients:

- 10 lbs. small, hard green tomatoes
- 1-1/2 lbs. red bell peppers
- 1-1/2 lbs. green bell peppers
- 2 lbs. onions
- 1/2 cup canning or pickling salt
- 1-quart water
- 4 cups sugar
- 1-quart vinegar (5%)
- 1/3 cup prepared yellow mustard
- 2 Tablespoons cornstarch

Directions:

a) Wash and coarsely grate or chop tomatoes, peppers, and onions. Dissolve salt in water and pour over vegetables in large kettle. Heat to boiling and simmer 5 minutes. Drain in colander. Return vegetables to kettle.

b) Add sugar, vinegar, mustard, and cornstarch. Stir to mix. Heat to boiling and simmer 5 minutes.

c) Fill hot sterile pint jars with hot relish, leaving 1/2-inch headspace.

d) Remove air bubbles and adjust headspace if needed. Wipe rims of jars with a dampened clean paper towel.

e) Adjust lids and process.

93. Pickled horseradish sauce

Ingredients:

- 2 cups (3/4 lb.) freshly grated horseradish
- 1 cup white vinegar (5%)
- 1/2 teaspoons canning or pickling salt
- 1/4 teaspoons powdered ascorbic acid

Directions:

a) The pungency of fresh horseradish fades within 1 to 2 months, even when refrigerated. Therefore, make only small quantities at a time.

b) Wash horseradish roots thoroughly and peel of brown outer skin. The peeled roots may be grated in a food processor or cut into small cubes and put through a food grinder.

c) Combine ingredients and ill into sterile jars, leaving 1/4-inch headspace.

d) Seal jars tightly and store in a refrigerator.

94. Pickled pepper-onion relish

Ingredients:

- 6 cups chopped onions
- 3 cups chopped sweet red peppers
- 3 cups chopped green peppers
- 1-1/2 cups sugar
- 6 cups vinegar (5%), preferably white distilled
- 2 Tablespoons canning or pickling salt

Directions:

a) Wash and chop vegetables. Combine all ingredients and boil gently until mixture thickens and volume is reduced by one-half (about 30 minutes).

b) Fill hot sterile jars with hot relish, leaving 1/2-inch headspace, and seal tightly.

c) Store in refrigerator and use within one month.

95. Spicy jicama relish

Ingredients:

- 9 cups diced jicama
- 1 Tablespoon whole mixed pickling spice
- 1 two-inch stick cinnamon
- 8 cups white vinegar (5%)
- 4 cups sugar
- 2 teaspoons crushed red pepper
- 4 cups diced yellow bell pepper
- 4-1/2 cups diced red bell pepper
- 4 cups chopped onion
- 2 fresh finger-hot peppers (about 6 inches each), chopped and partially seeded

Directions:

a) Caution: Wear plastic or rubber gloves and do not touch your face while handling or cutting hot peppers. Wash, peel and trim jicama; dice.

b) Place pickling spice and cinnamon on a clean, double-layer, 6-inch-square piece of 100% cotton cheesecloth.

c) Bring corners together and tie with a clean string. (Or use a purchased muslin spice bag.)

d) In a 4-quart Dutch oven or saucepot, combine pickling spice bag, vinegar, sugar, and crushed red pepper. Bring to boiling, stirring to dissolve sugar. Stir in diced jicama, sweet peppers, onion and finger-hots. Return mixture to boiling.

e) Reduce heat and simmer, covered, over medium-low heat about 25 minutes. Discard spice bag. Fill relish into hot pint jars, leaving 1/2-inch headspace. Cover with hot pickling liquid, leaving 1/2-inch headspace.

f) Remove air bubbles and adjust headspace if needed. Wipe rims of jars with a dampened clean paper towel.

g) Adjust lids and process.

96. Tangy tomatillo relish

Ingredients:

- 12 cups chopped tomatillos
- 3 cups chopped jicama
- 3 cups chopped onion
- 6 cups chopped plum-type tomatoes
- 1-1/2 cups chopped green bell pepper
- 1-1/2 cups chopped red bell pepper
- 1-1/2 cups chopped yellow bell pepper
- 1 cup canning salt
- 2 quarts water
- 6 Tablespoons whole mixed pickling spice
- 1 Tablespoon crushed red pepper lakes (optional)
- 6 cups sugar
- 6-1/2 cups cider vinegar (5%)

Directions:

a) Remove husks from tomatillos and wash well. Peel jicama and onion. Wash all vegetables well before trimming and chopping.

b) Place chopped tomatillos, jicama, onion, tomatoes, and all bell peppers in a 4-quart Dutch oven or saucepot. Dissolve canning salt in water. Pour over prepared vegetables. Heat to boiling; simmer 5 minutes.

c) Drain thoroughly through a cheesecloth-lined strainer (until no more water drips through, about 15 to 20 minutes).

d) Place pickling spice and optional red pepper lakes on a clean, double-layer, 6 inch-square piece

97. No sugar added pickled beets

Ingredients:

- 7 lbs. of 2- to 2-1/2-inch diameter beets
- 4 to 6 onions (2- to 2-1/2-inch diameter), if desired
- 6 cups white vinegar (5 percent)
- 1-1/2 teaspoons canning or pickling salt
- 2 cups Splenda
- 3 cups water
- 2 cinnamon sticks
- 12 whole cloves

Directions:

a) Trim of beet tops, leaving 1 inch of stem and roots to prevent bleeding of color. Wash thoroughly. Sort for size.

b) Cover similar sizes together with boiling water and cook until tender (about 25 to 30 minutes). Caution: Drain and discard liquid. Cool beets.

c) Trim of roots and stems and slip of skins. Slice into 1/4-inch slices. Peel, wash and thinly slice onions.

d) Combine vinegar, salt, Splenda®, and 3 cups fresh water in large Dutch oven. Tie cinnamon sticks and cloves in cheesecloth bag and add to vinegar mixture.

e) Bring to a boil. Add beets and onions. Simmer

f) 5 minutes. Remove spice bag. Fill hot beets and onion slices into hot pint jars, leaving 1/2-inch headspace. Cover with boiling vinegar solution, leaving 1/2-inch headspace.

g) Remove air bubbles and adjust headspace if needed. Wipe rims of jars with a dampened clean paper towel.

h) Adjust lids and process.

98. Sweet pickle cucumber

Ingredients:

- 3-1/2 lbs. of pickling cucumbers
- boiling water to cover sliced cucumbers
- 4 cups cider vinegar (5%)
- 1 cup water
- 3 cups Splenda®
- 1 Tablespoon canning salt
- 1 Tablespoon mustard seed
- 1 Tablespoon whole allspice
- 1 Tablespoon celery seed
- 4 one-inch cinnamon sticks

Directions:

a) Wash cucumbers. Slice 1/16th-inch of the blossom ends and discard. Slice cucumbers into 1/4-inch thick slices. Pour boiling water over the cucumber slices and let stand 5 to 10 minutes.

b) Drain of the hot water and pour cold water over the cucumbers. Let cold water run continuously over the cucumber slices, or change water frequently until cucumbers are cooled. Drain slices well.

c) Mix vinegar, 1 cup water, Splenda® and all spices in a 10-quart Dutch oven or stockpot. Bring to a boil. Add drained cucumber slices carefully to the boiling liquid and return to a boil.

d) Place one cinnamon stick in each empty hot jar, if desired. Fill hot pickle slices into hot pint jars, leaving 1/2-inch headspace. Cover with boiling pickling brine, leaving 1/2-inch headspace.

e) Remove air bubbles and adjust headspace if needed. Wipe rims of jars with a dampened clean paper towel.

f) Adjust lids and process.

99. Sliced dill pickles

Ingredients:

- 4 lbs. (3- to 5-inch) pickling cucumbers
- 6 cups vinegar (5%)
- 6 cups sugar
- 2 Tablespoons canning or pickling salt
- 1-1/2 teaspoons celery seed
- 1-1/2 teaspoons mustard seed
- 2 large onions, thinly sliced
- 8 heads fresh dill

Directions:

a) Wash cucumbers. Cut 1/16-inch slice of blossom end and discard. Cut cucumbers in 1/4-inch slices. Combine vinegar, sugar, salt, celery, and mustard seeds in large saucepan. Bring mixture to boiling.

b) Place 2 slices of onion and 1/2 dill head on bottom of each hot pint jar. Fill hot jars with cucumber slices, leaving 1/2-inch headspace.

c) Add 1 slice of onion and 1/2 dill head on top. Pour hot pickling solution over cucumbers, leaving 1/4-inch headspace.

d) Remove air bubbles and adjust headspace if needed. Wipe rims of jars with a dampened clean paper towel.

e) Adjust lids and process.

100. Sliced sweet pickles

Ingredients:

- 4 lbs. (3- to 4-inch) pickling cucumbers

Brining solution:

- 1 quart distilled white vinegar (5%)
- 1 Tablespoon canning or pickling salt
- 1 Tablespoon mustard seed
- 1/2 cup sugar

Canning syrup:

- 1-2/3 cups distilled white vinegar (5%)
- 3 cups sugar
- 1 Tablespoon whole allspice
- 2-1/4 teaspoons celery seed

Directions:

a) Wash cucumbers and cut 1/16 inch of blossom end, and discard. Cut cucumbers into 1/4-inch slices. Combine all ingredients for canning syrup in a saucepan and bring to boiling. Keep syrup hot until used.

b) In a large kettle, mix the ingredients for the brining solution. Add the cut cucumbers, cover, and simmer until the cucumbers change color from bright to dull green (about 5 to 7 minutes). Drain the cucumber slices.

c) Fill hot jars, and cover with hot canning syrup leaving 1/2-inch headspace.

d) Remove air bubbles and adjust headspace if needed. Wipe rims of jars with a dampened clean paper towel.

e) Adjust lids and process.

CONCLUSION

This cookbook contains many new research-based recommendations for canning safer and better quality food at home. It is an invaluable resource book for persons who are canning food for the first time. Experienced canners will find updated information to help them improve their canning practices.

www.ingramcontent.com/pod-product-compliance
Lightning Source LLC
Chambersburg PA
CBHW071602080526
44588CB00010B/989